Pilgrims' Steps

A Search for Spain's Santiago and an
Examination of his Way

Robert Hodum

iUniverse, Inc.
Bloomington

Pilgrims' Steps
A Search for Spain's Santiago and an Examination of his Way

iUniverse books may be ordered through booksellers or by contacting:

iUniverse
1663 Liberty Drive
Bloomington, IN 47403
www.iuniverse.com
1-800-Authors (1-800-288-4677)

Because of the dynamic nature of the Internet, any web addresses or links contained in this book may have changed since publication and may no longer be valid. The views expressed in this work are solely those of the author and do not necessarily reflect the views of the publisher, and the publisher hereby disclaims any responsibility for them.

Any people depicted in stock imagery provided by Thinkstock are models, and such images are being used for illustrative purposes only.

Certain stock imagery © Thinkstock.

ISBN: 978-1-4759-4012-1 (sc)
ISBN: 978-1-4759-4014-5 (e)
ISBN: 978-1-4759-4013-8 (dj)

Library of Congress Control Number: 2012913922

Printed in the United States of America

iUniverse rev. date: 10/15/2012

Acknowledgments

We shall not cease from exploration
And the end of all our exploring
Will be to arrive where we started
And know the place for the first time.
Through the unknown, the remembered gate
when the last of earth left to discover
Is that which was the beginning;
T.S. Elliot, 'Little Gidding', *Poetry 1900 to 1965*, ed. G. Macbeth (1967), p. 101

My profound thanks to my family whose love and support accompanied me on this journey. May we be ever mindful of the twists and turns of our paths along the Way!

My special thanks to Kim Harvey for her logo design and to Maria José Lloréns for the front and back cover photos. All interior black and white photos by Robert Hodum.

My sincere appreciation to those of you who have accepted my invitation to peer into the shadows of Spain's past, and examine one of her most cherished icons.

May Spain never abandon Santiago, and may his light continue to shine on Spain. May he walk beside each of us along the *Way*!

And as my Irish Grandpa John would say, "May joy and peace surround us, contentment latch our door, and happiness be with us now and bless us all evermore."

Table of Contents

The Master Returns Home

And the promised splendour
Breaks into the evening of the last stage of the journey,
Which almost exhales the fragrance of regret.
Raymoind Oursel, *Les pelegrins du moyen age: les hommes, les chemins, les*
sanctuaries (1963), cited in Horton and Marie-Helen Davies, *Holy Days and*
Holidays (1982), p. 210

The rías of Galicia broke through the cloud-enshrouded horizon
on the morning of the master's return. The journey began after a
clandestine departure from the Roman-controlled port city of Joppa.
His disciples had reclaimed his head and decapitated body from the
refuse dump beyond the west wall of Herod Agrippa's city. A royal
edict decreed that his body be exposed to the elements following the
afternoon execution, and be denied the ritual washing and predusk
burial which practice required. The master's followers removed the
remains under the new moon, ritually washed and wrapped them,
and then arranged for passage to the coast.

The transport of the late apostle would be completed before dawn.
His disciples hoped for anonymity among the matutinal bustle of
Joppa's docks; the apostle's remains sequestered under a wax-coated
canvas. Surrounded by provisions for the perilous spring journey, they
cast off. Their departure went unnoticed among the numerous fishing
boats setting out that morning. The creaking of wooden oars, the
slapping of unfurling canvass and the protests of the local fishermen
who strained casting their nets over the water's surface muted the
prayers of the unseasoned seamen. His disciples' vessel would follow
the Mediterranean's first century mercantile route to the west.

The crew would claim that divine intervention turned their rudder
and filled their sail as they slipped past Roman port garrisons and
sea patrols. They followed the coastline, passing the lands of Cyprus
and Crete, and sailed through the Straights of Malta. After having
charted a course around the islands of Sardinia and Corsica, down
past the Balearic Islands of Mallorca and Ibiza, the voyagers would
anchor in the ample harbor of Nova Cartago to take on fresh water
and food, and then set sail south. The water's roll off the Iberian
Levante would become more pronounced as they sailed towards the

Pillars of Hercules. They traversed the straits without incident and anchored in the ancient port city of Gades.

Their faces were unfamiliar to the Phoenician merchants who resupplied them for the final stretch of their voyage. Gades had been a frontier port of call a millennium before the birth of their martyred leader; its dancing girls heralded throughout the Mediterranean basin. Frequented by pirates and adventurers, this bustling city lay southeast of the ruins of the fabled city state of Tartessus where the famed Heracles once walked. The sights and happenings of this borderland settlement would be the disciples' last contact with the remnants of the known world. The darkness of the Western Ocean stretched before them.

Though traveled for centuries by fair-skinned northerners, Lusitanians, and the Ancient Sea People, the Atlantic still held dangers for sea-savvy mariners. Locals told stories of the unpredictable, sun swallowing waters of the western sea. The Celtic tribes of the Iberian Peninsula named this expanse of water the Land of the Dead. The master's disciples would do their best to dismiss these tales by remembering the sounds of their neighborhood streets and the voices of their families and friends. Perhaps they recalled a friendly face and the smells of the local markets of their native Galilee. They prayed that they would soon touch land again. As they ventured out into the ocean's waves, which rumbled and broke along the western coast of the peninsula of Roman Hispania, they must have wondered whether their journey was well advised. The master's crew proceeded north within sight of the rocky bluffs of the Iberian coastline, the land of the Lusitanians. Ever moving northward, their journey was almost complete.

Weary from weeks of tight quarters and the infrequent, yet, inevitable squabbles, the disciples searched the coastline for landmarks. They took heart as they passed the bay fed by the waters of the River Tagus, which led inland to the city of Scallabis, Lusitania's last river port. Their journey neared its end as they entered the waters of Gallaecia. They would have been unaccustomed to the lingering morning chill, so typical of the waters along the northwest corner of the Peninsula. The first night of the new moon would be their last on board. In the morning, they would head to the coast, sailing inland south of the Celtic ruins of Finisterra, into the frigid waters of the Galician drowned river valleys, the ría Noela, the namesake of the daughter of the biblical Noah. Here they would encounter the kingdom of Queen Lupa, the keeper of Lug's field of stars, the Celtic god of light.

Sailing to the headwaters of the ría, they cast anchor and came ashore, struggling to unload their invaluable cargo. Their master had arrived home. This was the land that he had walked almost a decade before. His dedicated followers, having ended their sea journey, traveled inland along the Roman highway, the Muxía Way. Many of these voyagers would evangelize the pagans of the northern outposts of Roman Tarraconensia. Some would return to Jerusalem with accounts of the distant land of the setting sun, where their master rested. His two most devoted followers, known as Athanasius and Theodore, remained to guard the tomb and convert the locals. They would follow their master into the mist of local legend and folklore.

Popular lore would recount that morning's legendary events long lost in time, immortalizing Jacob bar Zebedee and his return to Spain. Thus, began the mythic journey of Spain's St. James the Greater, the Apostle of Compostela. The stars over his burial ground would name his resting place, Campus Stella, marking this site for rediscovery by a shepherd monk several generations later. Jacob bar Zebedee, martyred Jew from a fishing village off the Sea of Galilee, would redefine Spain's spiritual identity. Pilgrimage to his tomb, aligned with St. James' celestial star field, the Milky Way, would become the nation's most enduring ritual, and he, its most enigmatic personage.

Author's Notes

*We have come purposely to a place, which seems marginal. Yet, the place of
solitude is only in appearance at the edge; in reality He is the one who stands at
the heart of things.*
Brother Ramon SSF, *The Heart of Prayer,* 1995, pg. 122

Santiago of Compostela, the biblical St. James the Greater, always
intrigued me. He was the divine savior of Christian Spain, who rested
in the crypt of the voluminous Compostela Cathedral in Galicia. As
an undergraduate who studied the chronicles of the Conquest of the
Americas, I first discovered the Santiago accounts during my stay
in Medellín, Colombia. Sanitago, the pilgrim saint and martyred
apostle, had become Santiago el Mataindios. Entreated by the Spanish
conquistadors as they engaged the Indigenous armies of Perú and
México, the multiple personage of St. James perplexed me. At first,
I considered him to be complicit in the Spanish rape of America, a
religious figure who legitimized the destruction of the indigenous
civilizations that I admired. I abjured all things Spanish and vowed
never to travel to Spain, nor would I become enamored of anything
or anyone Spanish; "never" was best never said.

Spain as the villain and ravager proved too simplistic a
characterization. My understanding of imperial Spain needed to be
depoliticized. The complexity of the conquistadors and the national
exigencies that drove Spain's Conquest of the Americas became
more contextual and comprehensible. It soon became clear, that to
understand Latin America I had to fathom Spain. And, of course, the
personage of Santiago de Compostela had to be reconsidered.

His presence in Spanish history always appeared anecdotal,
yet tied to pivotal historical events. Though he was inextricably
linked to Spain, and one of its most crucial periods of history, the
Reconquest, his presence in Spanish history appeared to be based
more on oral tradition and folklore than actual events. Perhaps, it was
his elusive nature coupled with my fascination with knights, chivalry,
religious miracles, and medieval castles that drew me closer to this
personage.

At times, the historical and fantastic seemed to corroborate the legendary Santiago of Compostela. History books reference accounts of St. James' divine intervention in defense of the besieged Christians, astride his luminescent steed riding into battle and vanquishing the infidel Moor. His burial in Spain and the pilgrimage to his crypt in the great cathedral of Compostela are textbook certainties. The medieval histories, hagiographies, and lectionaries that recounted the saint's biography intrigued me. Yet, I always felt dissatisfied with information about St. James, and suspected that another life story, perhaps even a grand mystery of sorts, might be teased out from these scant, biographical details.

I hesitate to qualify as actual the popular accounts of St. James' life, and thus, I refer to them as legendary history. The inconsistencies between the historical record and popular national belief, as well as the paucity of written documents about St. James, make an accurate reconstruction of his life challenging. Conjecture and extrapolation are not the cornerstones of sound historical analysis, but in cases such as these, threads must be sewn together to cloak and give shape to this historical figure.

This is not an attempt to present the definitive history of the saint, but instead provide insight into his diverse and complex persona. I consider this to be an examination of James' life and times, his family and their connections to religious and political movements of their day, as well as an overview of pre-Christian beliefs and lore from which this figure's legendary history certainly came.

A number of questions drove this work. Who was the actual James who figured so prominently in the accounts of Spanish history, and yet appeared so furtively in biblical records? Where might he have lived and what faith could he have practiced? Who were his parents and what relationship did they have with the family of Jesus? What cultural and historical antecedents preceded the Christian presence and their medieval pilgrimage? Did the beliefs of those ancient peoples figure in the development of this apostle's legendary history? Was he tied to a deeper, more profound tradition of sacred landscape and ancient line walking? The biographical information and the historical and cross cultural analysis that I've assembled, attempt to address these concerns. I interpret and draw conclusions that some may find fascinating, others curious, and a few might find this offensive and spurious. So be it!

I endeavor to connect the dots and draw a clearer image of his iconic figure. One has to sound the depths of myth and lore of Galicia, and beliefs of its ancient inhabitants to understand who the legendary James was. Only by sounding those depths, will we have a clearer picture of the historical Santiago. It is paramount that we understand that the historical counterpart of the legendary James, Spain's most revered Catholic icon, was Jacob bar Zebedee, a Jew who practiced a form of ascetic Judaism that was popular in Judea during the first century. An examination of the Santiago narrative falls short, if it fails to include its namesake's Jewish roots and beliefs. It is no small irony that Catholic Spain, while attempting to expunge that very presence from its social fabric, enshrined a Jew as the nation's patron saint.

St. James and his Way present a complex mosaic of ancient cultures and their religious beliefs. James' story is replete with conflicting medieval, archival, and folkloric accounts. The Church's exigencies downplayed the route's sacred landscape and highlighted the official destination; the relics entombed in the Cathedral of Compostela. Man's primordial reverence for the night sky and the terrain over which he walked and hunted must be reintegrated, and figure in a deeper understanding of the Santiago history as well as that of his Way.

A mythic undercurrent predates the presence of Christianity in the Iberian Peninsula. The routes to contemporary Compostela were traveled in prehistoric times and figured in ritualized pilgrimage activity. The ancient people who inhabited the north of Spain fused the terrain of the Way with their understanding of the sacred. St. James' legendary history incorporates their pre-Christian imagery and beliefs. He is discernible through the prism of the multitude of religious beliefs and histories of the peoples of the Iberian Peninsula. Santiago is not merely an amalgam of deities worshiped by early peoples of the northwest of Spain or other mythic figures of the ancient world. His legendary history is not limited to portrayals in accounts of regional quaint folklore. Although James stands as the national champion who rose during the conflict between Muslim and

Christian, he is not simply Santiago el Matamoros, but ultimately much more.

St. James might never have traveled through Spain, nor evangelized the pagan populations of Galicia as some Church hagiographies claim. His remains might not occupy the crypt in Compostela, but rather lie in Galilee, his birthplace, or in an unmarked grave in Jerusalem. Today's pilgrimage route parallels a pre-Christian sacred Way dedicated to Celtic and pre-Celtic gods. The ancient currents run deep through those fields, valleys and mountain passes. This might offend many who venerate him and seek his intercession. It has never been my intention to undermine belief in Spain's Santiago, or discredit the accounts of his life. In today's world faith is an absolute necessity. As a believer, I have been challenged to distinguish between what might have been Santiago's actual history, and the legend and myth that surround him. I have found that intermediary point that provides me with a satisfactory balance between my need to know and to believe. I wish you well in finding yours.

The ultimate challenge asks us to continue to be faithful in spite of what research and logic might reveal. It has been said that knowledge is death: death to ignorance and superstition, doctrine and orthodoxy. But ultimately, knowledge is an invitation to find a deeper meaning in all things historic. Standing before us is the whispered invitation to examine the semblance of man's mythological past that waits behind the mask of all things factual. Perhaps, we might glimpse our original face.

Writing this book was my first pilgrimage. Others have followed, giving me a keener appreciation of Man's need to touch the divine, and a deeper understanding of how the sacred imbues geography. After all, unraveling the enigma of St. James the Greater is as much a journey of faith as an intellectual endeavor.

Introduction

Spain's Santiago de Compostela

Good thoughts his only friends,
His wealth a well-spent age,
The earth his sober Inne,
And quiet Pilgrimage.
Thomas Campion, *The Works of Thomas Campion,* ed. W. Davies (1969), p.43

Spain is a country of celebrations. Rare is the town, city or region that does not honor its saints, commemorate some unique historical personage or celebrate the seasonal harvest. The festal and ritual calendars of Spain have always provided this nation with a depth and richness characteristic of few countries. A myriad of local, village-based holidays and festivals forms the basis of Spain's yearly ritual cycle. These local festivals, romerías, and holidays that originally focused on local virgin cults, patron saints, harvest events, and personages, once unknown beyond their villages or valleys, today form an extensive, national festal network.

Spain's festal calendar encompasses multitudinous, regional celebrations whose current popularity reaches beyond provincial boundaries, acquiring a national, and, in some cases, international notoriety. The growing popularity of the Valencian *Fallas*, Alicante's *Carnaval*, the tauromachia of Pamplona's *San Fermín* and Buñol's *Tomatina* have transcended their provincial settings and regional origins. These celebrations figure prominently in the nation's self-identity, and enjoy international recognition as being integral to Spain's current cultural reality.

Pilgrimage to St. James' tomb has marked Spanish ritual life for a dozen centuries. Although not a component of the annual festal calendar or an obligatory social ritual of the Spanish life-cycle such as baptism and communion, pilgrimage has become a widely shared experience among contemporary Spaniards. Regardless of age, political persuasion, and religious affiliation, nationalities from around the world have joined Spanish pilgrims to walk the Way to the legendary tomb of Santiago of Compostela, Spain's St. James.

The recent popularity of the *Way* to Compostela and its figurehead, St. James the Greater, invites further investigation of the origins of this ritual pilgrimage as well as the history of the route and its landscape. An in-depth examination of the biography of the man who has inspired such devotion requires us to widen our investigative scope beyond the medieval hagiographies and lectionaries. An interpretation of St. James' life must reflect on the historical and cosmological precursors to his pilgrimage pathway and place him in the sacro-historical continuum of which he is clearly a part. Dozens of centuries' use of the sacred route that reflects the star field of the Milk Way, flows back into Spain's pre-Christian past. Ancient peoples linked their cosmologies to Iberia's northern terrain and its night skies. The myths and legends surrounding Spain's Santiago give insight into the depth of the ancient mythological pool from which the St. James narrative draws. His legendary history continues the ancient amalgamation of the pathway's topography and Galicia's star fields, connecting Man to the sacred.

Textual support for examining the life of St. James is limited to New Testament references and lectionaries and hagiographies of the Middle Ages. Commentaries and reflections on the life of St. James the Greater must also include a study of his parents, the nature of the Judaism of his time and the particulars of the Essene sect to which he very likely belonged. Lastly, an understanding of the cultural and spiritual precursors to the Christian presence in the Peninsula is critical to fathoming Spain's St. James.

Santiago de Compostela, in the region of Galicia located in northwestern Spain, has been the center of the religious cult of St. James since the 9th century. Pilgrimage to the Cathedral of Compostela along the Way of St. James, also called the *Milky Way*, flourished in the 10th and 11th centuries when Pope Leo III declared this site *appropriate for veneration*. The route's history runs deeper than the legend of its most recent namesake, James the Greater, devoted follower of Jesus and one of Christianity's earliest apostle martyrs. Secondary routes of pilgrimage through Portugal, northern Africa, southern Spain, and southeastern France funneled millions of pilgrims during the Middle Ages to the city of Compostela, the recognized burial site of *Sant Yago*. This former Roman province of *Gallaecia* became the terminus for Christian pilgrimages, and ultimately, the source of national inspiration.

The search for the mythic and historical Santiago de Compostela requires a sounding of the legendary depths of his ritual pathway that spans dozens of centuries, numerous cultures, and their various faiths. Countless pilgrims have shared the sacred venue and its parallel star field over the course of millennia.This route was traversed long before humankind had a conscious understanding of the importance of pilgrimage. Migratory herds hunted by Neanderthal populations that inhabited the northwestern stretches of the Iberian Peninsula may have run the route from the ocean's coastline to the Mediterranean Sea. Small groups of Cro-Magnon hunters may have journeyed east along the pathway to grottos in the Pyrenean region of southeastern France for annual spring hunting rituals. An abundance of monolithic architecture near the pathway signifies the importance of the Way's terrain and its star fields in the cosmology of the Bronze Age populations in northern Spain. Its terminus, the Atlantic, brought ancient man to the threshold between his terra cognita and the challenge and mystery of the great expanse of ocean.

Celtic tribes who settled in this region in the 7th century BC named the watery expanse of the Atlantic the *Land of the Dead.* The Romans watched with *mysterium tremendum* as the light of the setting sun disappeared beneath its waves, building temples and cemeteries facing the landless extension to the west. Decimo July Brutus, Roman legionary, observed that the setting sun made a hissing sound similar to an iron when it is tempered in a forge. The Moors denominated it the *Terrible Sea.*

Although this route was known as el *Camino de Santiago* in the 12th and 13th centuries, pre-Christian populations walked it for millennia in search of spiritual enlightenment. Named the *Route of Stars*, the ancient pathway led out of the Pyrenees from southern France, along the coastline of the Bay of Biscay, through natural settings considered sacred by the Celtic tribes of this region, past today's Christian shrine in Compostela, and culminated at the rocky bluffs of Finisterre, overlooking the expanse of the Atlantic Ocean. Spain's ancient *Pathway of Light or Route of the Stars*, Via Lactea, dedicated to the Celtic sun deity Lugh (the Welsh *Lleu*, Gaelic *Lugos*), led to spiritual illumination and ritualized death and rebirth.

Pilgrims' Steps: A Search for Spain's Santiago and an Examination of his Way offers an interpretation of the history behind the shrine and its roots in pre-Christian spiritual activity and symbology and an examination of their historical namesake, St. James the Greater. It also provides personal reflections for those who carry this book along its sun-bleached routes and tree-enshrouded paths as well as for those who might never rise to that occasion. The history of St. James, Santiago of Compostela, contains narratives, which emerge from an ancient historical reality and find voice in legendary accounts based on popular histories and cross-cultural lore. The *Way* embodies the fulfillment of a pilgrimage route tied to sacred terrain shared by prehistoric man, ancient Bronze Age peoples, early Christians, pilgrims of the Middle Ages, and today's faithful. To do pilgrimage to Compostela is to be a part of all of this. The Way's valleys and hills, tree enshrouded paths and streams continue to connect humanity with the celestial divide and return us to ourselves as we find a place in the firmament here on Earth

Ultimately, the cult of Santiago finds expression in a mythic narrative that transcends current religious configuration and speaks to a universal, millenniums-old interior voice. Santiago's sacred route takes humanity to a threshold veiled by a mosaic of lore and myth. It invites us to a more intimate solidarity with our past, and with ourselves. The waters of his mountain streams and verdant hillocks dispel the disquiet of our world, whispering to us that we are finally home.

Pilgrims' peace of St. James
Swallows' flight unseen
In the light of a pale moon passing,
Let fall life's stones of blame, guilt,
And years of disbelief
Along this road that pulls us forward.
Leave angry words, mistrust
And yearnings ill conceived
In the shadows along the Way this eve.
And find pilgrims' peace in Santiago.

Robert Hodum
7/25/2007

Inspired by Luis Pastor and Joao Alfonso

Chapter 1
JACOB BAR ZEBEDEE: THE
SANTIAGO OF SPAIN

James is Jacob of the House of Zebedee
Reflection: People are much more than we believe them to be.

We would true valour see, let him come hither;
One here will constant be, come wind, come weather
There's no discouragement shall make him once relent
His first avow'd intent, to be a pilgrim.
John Bunyan, *The Pilgrim's Progress*, 1678

Saint James the Greater, Spain's Santiago de Compostela, was one of the original apostles. His Hebrew name was Jacob bar Zebedee. The historical Jacob of the house of Zebedee was born near the lakeside town of Tiberias. His father, Zebedee, and mother, Mary Helena (Herena) Salomé, a cousin of Mary, the mother of Jesus, like many Jews of their time, named their first son after Jacob, the ancestor of the Israelites. The brothers Zebedee left their parents and became the first followers of Jesus. James, identified as one of Jesus' favorite apostles in the New Testament, attended the reviving of the dead daughter of Jarius, personally witnessed the transfiguration of Jesus on Mount Tabor, and accompanied Christ in the Garden of Gethsemane. (Thurston & Attwater, *Butler's Lives of the Saints*, 182)

Jacob bar Zebedee and his brother, John, later known as the Evangelist, lived in a crowded community of more than ten thousand, located on the shore of one of the nine *beth-saida* or fisher-home townships. They fished the waters of the Sea of Galilee with their cousins Peter and Andrew. Their community, located along a stretch of the ancient trade routes between Egypt and Mesopotamia, Syria and Greece, thrived. These Galilean settlements founded on the northern slopes of the cliffs and hills of the landlocked Sea of Galilee dotted the bowl of the Rift Valley. Hot springs and the River Jordan fed the waters of Galilee and provided a fertile setting for a thriving fishing industry. Sailors and anglers of this region depended on the West Wind that blew down through the plain of *Gennesaret* to Galilee's rich fishing grounds and occasioned unpredictable wintry winds and sudden summer squalls. Jacob came to adulthood in this setting.

Excavations located a *beth-saida* settlement, some 1.5 miles from the Sea of Galilee. (*Biblical Archaeology*, July/August, 1998) Originally located on the shores of the Sea, the settlement was reportedly the home of Simon Peter, Andrew and Philip. This site, abandoned in antiquity after an earthquake and frequent flooding, may have been the venue for Jesus' miracles of the feeding of the multitudes, the healing of the blind and Jesus' walking on water. Flavius Josephus, the historian and Zealot general, fought an important battle against the Romans near this site during the First Jewish Revolt of 66-70 AD. Some believe that Herod Agrippa I excommunicated Zebedee, father of Jacob, for his participation in this very conflict.

Although Jacob and his brother, John, formed part of an inner circle among the twelve disciples, New Testament scripture indicates that Jesus rebuked them for their intemperate and mercurial nature. Traditional sources note that James and his brother were known as the tempestuous ones, hence their appellation, *Boanerges*, interpreted by Mark as "sons of thunder". *Butler's Lives of the Saints* interprets this phrase, not dissimilar to other traditional sources, as reflecting their "impetuous spirit and fiery tempers". (Thurston & Attwater, *Butler's Lives of the Saints*, 182) Jacob and John, zealous supporters of Christ, suggested that the unresponsive inhabitants of a Samarian town be punished with consuming heavenly fire,

> "Lord, wilt Thou that we bid fire come down from heaven and consume them?" (Luke 9, 51-56)

The title, *boanerges,* might not have spoken to the brothers' ill humor and fanaticism, but rather their family's position and influence in the Essene community. Their title "sons of thunder" might be better understood through an examination of Jacob bar Zebedee's parents and the religion they practiced.

Jacob was born into a family of considerable visibility in the Essene community, whose sanctuary was situated at the Monastery of Mird, south of Jerusalem. His family very likely belonged to the Nazorean or Nazarene sect of the Essenes. Jacob would have adopted the beliefs of his parents and would have been considered inheritor of his father's status in this ascetic, religious community. The Essenes embraced a Gnostic tradition whose practices included astrology, healing, asceticism, and celibacy, much of which could be traced to a non-Judaic origin. [1]

A counterbalance of Light and Darkness formed the nexus of the Essene cosmological vision. This duality was made incarnate by two influential ministers of the Sanctuary and prominent figureheads in the religious hierarchy of the Essene community, who vied for hegemony in local political issues as well as spiritual ones. Zebedee, Jacob's father, was a prominent figure in this religious community. As a minister of the sanctuary he would have participated in ceremonies that symbolized the struggle between the cosmic forces of Light and Darkness. Zebedee may have held the position of *Lightning,* serving as counterpoint to the rival *Thunder* party, headed by Jonathan, son of Ananus, a Sadducee High Priest. Jacob and his younger brother, John, came to age in this political setting. The brothers Zebedee might have become affiliated with or attempted to form an alliance between

---

[1] Wallace-Murphy and Hopkins in their work *Rosslyn: Guardian of the Secrets of the Holy Grail* write that precursors to Essene beliefs may be found in the teachings of Melchizedek, which were popular in Galatia and Asia Minor, as well as the Druidic spiritual tradition.

these groups, and thus, were known as the sons of *Boanerges*, the spiritual sons of Thunder and Lightning.

Zebedee was described as a man of relative wealth, of good standing in his community, and possessed of considerable business acumen. St. Jerome indicates that James' family was from Haifa and "of noble origin." (Starkie, *The Road to Santiago*, 13) Perhaps this speaks to his family ties with Jesus, heir to King David's throne. In *Butler's Lives of the Saints*, his father is identified as a fisherman by trade, who lived with his two sons and wife on the shores of Genesareth. His partnership with the sons of Jonah of *Bethsaida Julias*, Andrew and Peter, appears to have been successful. Together they packed and distributed salted fish to the ten townships surrounding the Sea of Galilee. This profitable family business might have employed some of the other apostles.

Some contend that Jacob's father was known as Simon Zelotes in the circle of militant Zealots and had been associated with an unsuccessful revolt during the rule of Pontius Pilate. Zebedee's political activism would lead to his excommunication by Herod Agrippa I. The enmity that developed between Agrippa and Jacob's father was long-standing. This bitter relationship ended in murder. Herod Agrippa I ordered the beheading of his oldest son, Jacob, making him the first martyred apostle of Jesus. Zebedee was credited with exacting vengeance by poisoning Herod Agrippa a year after his son's execution.

Mary Helena Salomé, Jacob's mother, might have occupied positions of importance in the Essene community and was possibly known by several names and titles. Recognized as the consort of Zebedee, she would have held the rank of High Priestess of the Order Asher, recognized as a woman well versed in sacred teachings. Mary Helena Salomé possessed the title of *Miriam* or *Mary,* a priestess who officiated at ceremonies and led the women of the Therapeutate Essene Community.[2] Susan Haskins in her study *Mary Magdalen: Myth and Metaphor* identifies the *Miriam* as women "who knew all and reveal the greatness of the revealer, the one who is the inheritor of Light."

---

[2] Wallace-Murphy and Hopkins present a unique interpretation of the relationship of the brothers Zebedee and Jesus. They maintain that after the death of Joseph, Mary, the mother of Jesus, marries Zebedee, making Jesus their half-brother.

Incarnate in their role was the position of privileged interlocutrix of the sacred knowledge of God. (Haskins, 35, 41, 47)

She, like the other women of her Order, would have worn the red robe which symbolized the knowledge of hidden truths. As such, she would have actively healed and taught according to the Nazarene tradition. Salomé was also seen as a strong advocate for her sons. She requested of Jesus that they sit with him when he claimed his throne. The other apostles, as St. Matthew states, condemned her forwardness saying, "…when the ten heard it, they were moved with indignation against the two brethren." (St. Matthew 20, 21-22) Walter Starkie qualifies Salomé as being "the prototype of an ambitious matron, mother of noble sons."(Starkie, *The Road to Santiago*, 19) Again, this reference to nobility speaks of their family's connection to the Nazarene. Perhaps it is indicative of their belief in a terrestrial throne to which they had claim.

Studies indicate the possibility that Anna, mother of Mary, lived in a region near a *beth-saida* pool and well, a site under Essene supervision. Proximity and use of these waters may have linked the family of Mary to this Jewish sect. Mary Helena Salomé, a member of the Essene community, is believed to have been the first cousin of Mary, and niece of Anna.

After the death of Jesus, various oral histories place Jacob's mother in different parts of the ancient world. One tradition maintains that after Jesus' death, Mary Helena Salomé accompanied Simon Zelotes/Zebedee to Cyprus, where they founded settlements based on the ascetic teachings of the Therapeutate from the ancient Essene community at Qumran.[3]

Another account of her final years places her with Mary Magdalen in southern France around 44 AD. The Magdalen, Salomé, and several other travelers would have followed the sea route of Jewish tin traders who regularly shipped ore from the port city of Marseilles. This group of women reportedly disembarked at Les Saintes Maries de la Mer in Provence. According to local tradition, Salomé traveled through the south of France with Mary Magdalen, reaching the ancient port of Masillia, contemporary Marseilles, France.[4]

---

[3] Bargil Pixner in *With Jesus in Jerusalem: His First and Last Days in Judea* (Rosh Pina, Israel: Corazin Publishing, 1996

[4] The actual burial place of Mary Magdalen remains a point of controversy given that

All accounts attest to Mary Helena Salomé's unswerving advocacy of her sons. She interceded on their behalf when she requested that Jesus, upon ascending his throne, allow her sons to sit at the right and left of him. Some have interpreted this as simply being an overly assertive and presumptuous mother. But, perhaps she sought to insure for her progeny what was rightfully theirs; a position of noble standing due to their family's link to the Davidic heir. Jesus responded by saying that humility, patience, and industry brought greater rewards than ambition and forwardness. When asked if they would drink of his cup, they responded affirmatively. Some would maintain that they were unaware of the suffering inherent in that act. Others would see their petition as an attempt to clarify their claim on a future throne. Their mother's request reveals a belief in the establishment of a terrestrial, temporal monarchy. Such a monarchy under the reign of their cousin, Jesus, would have been more than a casual interest to them.

Jacob's brother was well known in his own right. John bar Zebedee, known as the Evangelist, would also be recognized as his father's spiritual and political heir. Recognized by the high priest's portress, he had access to the inner courtyard of the palace of Annas and Caphias, and reportedly supplied the royal family with fresh fish. Polycrates, a bishop of Ephesus, indicated John's familiarity with the high priest of Jerusalem:

"Simon Peter followed Jesus and so did another disciple. As this disciple was known to the high priest, he entered the court along with Jesus, while Peter stood outside the door." (John 18: 15-16).

Jacob's younger brother had been given access to the trial of Jesus. Archival evidence does not place Jacob on Calvary, but John reportedly witnessed the death of Jesus, and comforted Mary at the foot of the cross.[5] Later, non-biblical, oral tradition indicates that

numerous dioceses claim to be the burial sites of the saint. The major French sites are Ste. Marie-Madeleine, Vélzelay, Burgundy or St. Maximin, Provence. Haskins indicates that the earliest claim to the body of Mary is made in Ephesus near the entrance of the Cave of the Seven Sleepers preceding all others by five hundred years

[5] As to which Mary this might have been is an issue that is open for discussion. The three prominent Marys of the New Testament figure in this scene. Mary, daughter of Anna (Anne), mother of Jesus, was present during his crucifixion. Mary, the Magdalen, Mary of the Towers, (Migdala - of the tower) follower and intimate confidant of Jesus, attended

Jacob had attended Jesus' execution along with his mother, Mary Helena Salomé.

The Origins of Jacob's Faith
Reflection: Ancient beliefs run beneath our feet.

It is a deliberate sundering and surrendering of one's habitual conditions of comfort, routine, safety and convenience ... the pilgrim breaks with his material servitude ... and sets out on a quest which is inward as much as outward, and which is, in varying degrees, into the unknown.
Social Anthology of Pilgrimage, ed. Makhan Jha (1991), p. 302

Judaism at the time of Jacob bar Zebedee was a product of evolution and transformation. The faith of his parents was the result of centuries of amalgamation and proscription. Their religion contained a spiritual esthetic that was as much a product of their contact with surrounding populations, as it was an attempt to distinguish themselves from their neighbors' visions of the divine.

The history of ancient Judaism is a study of exclusion and inclusion of elements from surrounding cultures and religions. The faith Jacob bar Zebedee practiced was a product of this religious dynamic. Judaism of the 1st century AD was the visage whose reflection is found subtly revealed in its offspring, Christianity.

The monotheistic precept so clearly identified with post-Babylonian Judaism circa 536 BC, found its formative stages among the peoples of Mesopotamia, and developed from a polytheistic setting. Sacred unions of gods and goddesses signified the marriage of sky and earth deities. Male sun gods such as the Canaanite *Bel/Baal* found solace in the arms of divine consorts and wives. Judaism of the 10th century BC was an amalgamation of gods, goddesses and fertility cults. (Susan Haskins, *Mary Magdalen: Myth and Metaphor*, 43)

The Sumerian, Assyrian, Babylonian and Canaanite cosmological visions had a clear male-female duality that incorporated sun gods and star goddesses. The essence of God was dualistic, and engendered as both male and female. *Ishtar* was worshipped by the Mesopotamians at Uruk, the Sumerian temple, *Astarte* in Syria and

his execution and Mary Helena Salomé, mother of Jacob and John, the Evangelist, was present. Salomé was believed to have left Palestine and lived at Les Saintes Marie de la Mer, in southern France. She was known by the name of Mary and was identified as Jesus' mother's sister.

Phoenicia, and *Ashtoreth* by the Canaanites. Divinities were united in sacred marriage; Astarte married Baal, god of the Canaanites, Ishtar was the lover of Tammuz, shepherd god of Mesopotamia, and Isis was the wife of Osiris in Egypt. Susan Haskins in her study *Mary Magdalen: Myth and Metaphor* comments on these sacred marriages and the reappearance of the Mother Goddess in ancient Middle Eastern religions. Haskins cites the prophet Hosea who intimated the existence of a male/female dyad in early Judaism and "saw Israel as Yahweh's faithless wife..." Inscriptions in Hebrew from the eighth century BC, discovered in the Negev desert, refer to "the Lord and his Asherah..." the name of the Canaanite goddess of fertility. (Haskins, 43)

The worship of *Ashtoreth*, the Canaanite star goddess, formed an integral part of the Israelite's view of the cosmos before the 6th century BC. Called *Asherah* by the Israelites, she, with the supreme male deity, *El*, formed the divine celestial couple. *Anath*, Queen of the Heavens, and *He*, King of the Heavens, were the progeny of their union. *El* and *He*, (father and son) evolved into a single male divinity, Yahweh. The female entities merged to form Shekinah or Matronit, consort to the supreme male deity, later known as Jehovah. YHWH represented the geometry of the original celestial family: Y represented El *the Father*; H, Asherah *the Mother*; W, He, *the Son*; and H, Anath, *the Daughter*. (Munro, *Glory Paths*, 93)

The eventual transformation of this celestial family into an amalgamated version that centered on two deities was the initial step toward the monotheism of Solomon. The female component, subjugated and eventually eliminated during this evolutionary process, appeared in the Phoenician architecture of the Great Temple of Solomon. Judaism's original proponent of monotheism, Solomon, upon the death of his father, David, sought out the help of Canaanite architects to the north. The construction of Solomon's Temple, attributed to Hiram of Tyre, follower of the goddess Astarte, contained elements of sacred architecture which characterized temples and sanctums dedicated to this female deity of the Canaanites. The inner sanctuary of ancient Judaism's architectural icon, the Holy of Holies, was identified with the womb of Ashtoreth.

Solomon's embrace of monotheism in the form of Yahweh was not to the exclusion among his subjects of popular animist, polytheistic sentiments. Many were proponents of a strong belief in the forces of nature and held a deep respect and acknowledgment of the significance of the female divine entity. The nascent monotheism of Judaism suffered frequent falls into polytheistic apostasy. Mircea Eliade in his work *The Sacred and the Profane: The Nature of Religion* commented that the ancient Jews frequently returned "to the Baals and the Astartes" and returned only to the single godhead during times of crisis. (126) Old Testament accounts speak to this struggle:

"And they cried unto the Lord, and said ... We have sinned for we have forsaken the Lord and have served Baalim and Ashtaroth, but now deliver us out of the hands of our enemies, and we will serve thee." (I Samuel, 1210)

Judaism distanced itself from the male/female duality of the polytheistic vision of her neighbors. At the time of Jacob bar Zebedee's formative years, Judaism had abandoned its original polytheistic, male-female dynamic, and had maintained a proscription of acts of worship of female entities such as those intimated at in the architecture of the Solomon's Temple. Judaism of the first century embraced elements of her neighbors' concepts of divinity and the cosmos. Its manuscripts and holy texts, scrolls and tractates chronicled not only the struggle of the Israelites against subjugation at the hands of surrounding cultures, their military exploits which sought to establish political hegemony for the Israelites, but also culminated in their belief in unified divinity of monotheism. Theological borrowings, self-definition and, eventually, the ethic of proscription and rites of passage, initiation, and esoteric insight came to form the religion of Jacob's community.

The dynamic of Judaism centered on the messianic promise of deliverance from foreign domination, the reconstitution of political hegemony, and the maintenance of the succession of the Davidic line. Minority sects continued to flourish as in the past. The ascetic ethic of one of the three principal Jewish sects of his time, the Essenes, was particularly attractive to Zealots and unaffiliated ascetics. Jacob, son of Zebedee, not unlike his immediate family and close relatives,

9

was profoundly influenced by the beliefs of the Essene community in Qumran.

The Light and Darkness of the Essenes
Reflection: Life is a commitment to a path.

The idea of pilgrimage is much older than Christianity. It has been an expression of the same two concepts; that of making a pilgrimage by traveling to a specific geographical site and that of being on a perpetual pilgrimage; the journey of life itself. Both are in pursuit of a greater good, and both involve discomfort and hardship.
Margaret Pawley, *Prayers for Pilgrims*, 1991, p. xiii

The Essenes, Pharisees and the Sadducees represented the three major factions of Judaism centuries before the birth of Jesus. The ascendency of the Maccabees after the successful uprising in 167 BC against Antiochus IV Epiphanes, the Seleucid emperor of Syria, signaled the reconsecration of the Temple. A major theological schism developed between the House of Maccabaeus and a small ultra-religious sect known as the *Hasidim,* who established their community in the Wilderness of Qumran, splitting from the mainstream of Judaism around 130 BC. Robert Eisenman comments in *James the Brother of Jesus* that a possible derivation of Essenes comes from the Aramaic meaning the Pious Ones, *Hasidim* in Hebrew. (Eisenman, 305)

The early Essene sect practiced an ascetic form of Judaism, which had bifurcated from the ancient Hasidim. These ascetics began building their Qumran settlement during the reign of John Hyrcanus in 135 BC. Many Nazarenes embraced the teachings of the Essene brotherhood who continued the ascetic traditions and strict interpretations of the law of the ancient Hasidim. They repopulated the early settlements, which had been abandoned after the devastating earthquake of 31 BC and lived in monastic settlements numbering around four thousand, meticulously observing the Torah. (Michael Grant, *History of Ancient Israel*, 218) The Qumran community's violent end proceeded the fall of Jerusalem in 70 AD. Caches of coins seem to indicate that use of the site continued into the time of the Second Jewish Revolt of 132 - 35 AD. (J.M. Allegro, *The Dead Sea Scrolls*, 85)

Josephus, a Jewish historian and contemporary of John the Baptist, stated that the Essenes claimed their exclusive right to the high-priesthood tradition. Influenced by the Hellenic principles of the immortality of the soul, they did not believe in the resurrection of the physical body. (Grant, *History of Ancient Israel*, 218) Jacob's parents practiced this particular form of Judaism, and very likely maintained relationships with prominent figures in the Essene religious community of Qumran. The Essene brotherhood's vision was apocalyptic and messianic. Their teachings focused on the bipolarity of Light and Darkness, of Good and Evil, indicative Persian and Hellenistic influences. (219) This cosmic battle, known as the doctrine of the *Two Spirits*, was played out daily in the hearts of the faithful as well as in a terrestrial military theater between "the Jews of Levite, Judahite and Benjamite ancestry and the forces of Edom, Moab, Ammon and Philistia on the one hand and the Kittim on the other." (Allegro, 121)

The Essenes were described as healers who had knowledge of ancient practices which included healing through the lying on of hands as well as the therapeutic use of minerals, plants and stones. They were students of the stars and the planets. Their vision of the cosmos centered on a world that counterbalanced truth and righteousness with evil and perversion, a world of Light and Darkness kept in equilibrium by celestial movement. Followers of astrology and students of astronomy, they believed that celestial movement affected the human condition and determined the extent to which this duality manifested itself in one's life. Life was a process of walking a path fraught with challenges and temptations.

The leader of the sect known as Zadok bore the title of the *Teacher of Righteousness,* and the members of the Qumran sect, called themselves Sons of Zadok. (Allegro, 95) The calendar of the Essenes, differing from Jerusalem's was based on the book of Jubilees that divided the year into 12 months with 52 weeks of 30 days each. Tuesday night marked the beginning of the Sabbath, and thus, the Essenes held Wednesday to be sacred. The books of Enoch and Jubilees written in Aramaic were the most popular manuscripts in the community's scriptorium. (Allegro, 116, 119)

The central core of Essene beliefs was based on an ascetic ethic of strict self-discipline. Their religious ethos underscored the need to balance the positive and negative forces encountered daily through prayer, self-privation and a personal commitment to seek righteousness. Celibacy and meal taking but once a day figured in the ascetic life style of the Essenes. Their knowledge of celestial occurrences and belief that representatives of these counterbalancing forces had a terrestrial manifestation formed the Essene world vision. They believed in the immortality of the spirit and that salvation would come to those who kept the faith and broke free from the flesh and worldly temptation by controlling their bodily needs. (Daniel Silver, *History of Judaism*, 245)

The Light, symbolized by the candlesticks of the menorah, was incarnate in the community's representative, the Zadokite priest who represented the Righteous One. The Chief of Scribes played the role of Darkness and provided a formal structural element of opposition in this religious and political duality. He was the tempter who tested initiates' understanding of the law, their adherence to its precepts, and the dedication of the female initiates to celibacy. The Darkness represented the ancient forces of *Belial* whose followers were polytheistic, and represented a return to Judaism's ancient past and the beliefs of its former neighbors.

The followers of the Essene sect were practiced in the art of allegorical phrases with coded vocabulary and expressions. They used special cryptic titles and designations for functionaries, priests, and titular heads. Their scribes used parables, allegories, and special terms which gave their writings dual levels of significance. Their terminology was resurrected from arcane biblical references, thus confining the message to the chosen, and denying access to the uninitiated. Paramount in these concerns was their subterfuge against the Romans whom they called *Kittim* and Rome *Babylon*. Their cryptic messages contained political denunciations of Rome's occupation, and their pseudonyms described titles and delineated standing in their Community. A member's political and social status was described in esoteric terms, which hinted at transcendent phenomena, yet enumerated basic political, religious and social responsibilities in the Essene community. The messianic component of the Essenes' cosmology allowed for a twin Messiahship; a priestly messiah whose realm was celestial and a kingly Davidic, terrestrial messiah. [6]

On a final and curious note an observation made by Josephus concerning Essene belief in the afterlife seems to tie the western horizon with the soul's resting place. Josephus described the ancient Mandaeans of Southern Iraq and Iran. These Essenes who left Jerusalem after Jesus' crucifixion believed that souls resided, "… Beyond the ocean to the west, in a region not oppressed with storms of rain snow or intense heat, but has refreshing gentle breezes. A star marks this wonderful place called Merica that sits in the sky above it."(*Second Messiah*, 106)

Coincidence has it that the tomb of a disciple of Jesus whose family very likely was either Essene or influenced by the Essene community's teachings is located according to tradition in the western-most corner of the Iberian Peninsula, Galicia. To what star or group of stars Merica might refer is a matter of conjecture. The light and stars of the *Via Lactea* are enduring components of the legendary history of St. James. Galicia is certainly not a land free of neither rain nor intemperate weather, but the western directionality of this spiritual domain, and the legendary resting-place of Jacob bar Zebedee, Spain's St. James, is intriguing.

---

[6] J.M. Allegro indicates that these two messiahs officiated at the sect's Messianic Banquet, one the High priest and the other lay or Davidic Messiah. (115) The twin Messiahship could be applied to the two most prominent figures of the New Testament, John the Baptist and Jesus. Numerous biblical scholars see the Baptist, first cousin to Jesus, as the priestly messiah whose kingdom was not terrestrial. Jesus has been portrayed as the King and terrestrial leader and the completion of the Davidic line. John the Baptist and Jesus were Levites as determined by their matrilineal lineage and were entitled to assume the duties of high priests and of entering the Holy of Holies.

Jacob's Presence in Hispania
Reflection: His footsteps might not have crossed this way.

Thou art a pilgrim as we are, this night thou fare as we fare,
Be it less or be it more Thou shall assay:
Then tomorrow thou prepare to wend thy way.
The Pilgrims, from *The Wakefield Mystery Plays*, ed. Martial Rose,
1961, pg. 409-10

It is highly unlikely that Jacob or any of the other apostles would have left Palestine soon after the crucifixion. The *Acts of the Apostles* indicates that they preached in the Holy Land, and although Peter assigned lands to evangelize to the remaining apostles, Jacob's early martyrdom in 44 AD would have prevented him from evangelizing outside of Palestine or of ever visiting the Iberian Peninsula.

The earliest efforts at evangelization in the Iberian Peninsula appear not to have predated the mid 50s, yet some set the date almost ten years earlier in the year 46. However, early Church archives indicate an absence of any substantial Christian presence in the Roman province of Hispania before 100 AD. Hispania, one of the western-most provinces of Rome, was divided into the two major regions; *Hispania Citerior* and *Hispania Ulterior,* separated by the course of the Ebro River. The five provinces of Tarraconesis, Lusitania, Carthaginensis, Baetica, and Gallaecia facilitated economic and military control of one of Rome's most lucrative and rebellious provinces. This province identified as one of its most rebellious was indeed a site of early Christian evangelization. It is believed that Peter sent missionaries to Baetica whose principal cities were *Hispalis-Italica* and *Corduba*, the contemporary Andalucian cities of Sevilla and Córdoba. The early Christians would have traveled to Lusitania, contemporary Portugal and western central Spain, and visited its major urban centers, *Emerita Augusta* (Mérida) and *Toletum*, (Toledo).

Paul may have been the first of Jesus' apostles to visit Spain, expressing an interest in visiting Spain in 63 nearly 21 years after Jacob's execution. (Rom. 15: 23- 28) His announcement to the Romans not to preach the gospel where "Christ had already been named lest he might build on another man's foundation" underscores the distinct possibility that Jacob had never traveled to Hispania. (Rom. 15: 23-28)

Paul, arrested in 61 and held captive for two years, might have visited Spain between 63 and 67 AD. If such a trip took place, Paul would have visited the western reaches of Tarraconensis, a region that corresponded to present-day Aragón, Navarra and Cataluña. If Paul had preached in the Iberian Peninsula, he would have entered through Tarraco, contemporary Tarragona. He would have traveled along the Via Ceasar Augusta, a highway that crossed central Hispania or down the Levante through Nova Cartago to Gades, Spain's Cádiz, visiting the most prominent Jewish synagogues of these cities.

Dale G. Vought in *Like a Flickering Flame* makes a very strong case for Paul's presence in Hispania. He cites Clement of Rome and Chrysostom who made reference to the apostle's presence in the Iberian Peninsula. In a letter to the church in Corinth in 69 AD, Clement of Rome indicates that Paul had taught "righteousness to the whole world, and had come to the extreme limit of the west ..." Hispania was the western most limit of the known world. Chrysostom makes direct references to Paul's presence in Spain stating, "For after he had been in Rome, he returned to Spain, but whether he came thence again into these parts, we know not." (Nicene and Post-Nicene Fathers, Series I Volume XIII (ECF -Volume XXII) F, on II Timothy 4:20, Paragraph 26)

M. Diaz y Diaz in his work *San Pablo en España* indicates that Paul's presence in Spain has significant textural support and should be given serious consideration. He contends:

"The evangelizing presence of Saint Paul in Hispania (Spain) seems to be beyond all reasonable doubt; the testimony, both contemporary and later, is conserved almost in its entirety in authors and texts unrelated to the Peninsula, and are therefore free of a biased interpretation, giving sufficient proof."
(San Pablo en España, Historia 16, ExtmXN, June 1980, pg.20)

The striking omission of St. James from the records of the early Church in Hispania calls into doubt the accounts of his legendary travels and presence in the Peninsula, undermining any historic actuality that their authors might claim. The major Spanish liturgical writers of the early Middle Ages from the 4th to the 8th centuries make no mention of St. James or his travels in Roman Hispania. Aurelio Clemente Prudencio, 348-405, and Idacio, the bishop of Aquae Flaviae, a diocese that bordered the legendary burial site in Gallaecia, failed to comment on his presence or activities. St. Jerome writes of Spain, yet makes no mention of James, the Greater. Other writings of the early Church attest to the fact that Jacob bar Zebedee lived and preached in Galilee and Samaria, and suffered martyrdom in Jerusalem.

The absence of archival support for Jacob's evangelizing in Roman Hispania undermines the veracity of numerous local histories, popular legends, and medieval hagiographies that maintain that Jacob evangelized in *Gallaecia* in the north of Hispania, traversed the northern provinces of the Iberian Peninsula, and traveled down the Ebro River through contemporary Aragón to the Mediterranean coast. After four years of failed evangelism, the apostle departed from the port of Tarraconesis, contemporary Tarragona, returned to Jerusalem, and joined a small enclave of Christians led by James the Lesser.

The theologian and historian Gregory de Tours, 538-594, wrote extensively on the holy sites and sanctuaries of Hispania and did not mention the shrine of James, the Greater. Pope Inocencio I chronicled the failed evangelistic efforts of the prelates of Hispania in the early 400's and made no accounting of the apostle James. Lastly, the bishop of Pointiers, Fortunato, when describing the evangelistic churches established by the original apostles, did not mention any specific sites in Hispania or St. James the Greater, our Jacob bar Zebedee. Saint Julian, Archbishop of Toledo in 686 denied in his work The Sixth Age that James had ever evangelized in Hispania, but rather placed him in Judea spreading the gospel among the Jews following the direction of James the Lesser.

A succession of 7th century Visigoth writers in Hispania, which included the historian and archivist, Saint Isidoro, the archbishop of Seville, continued to question the apostle's presence and participation in the evangelization of the Peninsula. Only one work of dubious authenticity attributed to this archbishop of Seville locates Jacob in

Hispania. Finally, Pope Clement VIII of the 16th century expunged all previous references to St. James's evangelizing in Hispania from the Brevarium. The scant historical records that address the life of Jacob bar Zebedee indicate that the apostle acted on a stage set in Judea, evangelized the Jews of this region, suffered martyrdom in Jerusalem, and was buried in Palestine.

Finally, worth noting is the contention that Spain's Santiago may never have existed at all. Robert Eiseman in his work *James the Brother of Jesus* postulates that James, the Greater was a fabrication to hide one of Jesus' siblings.[7]

The Early Church in Hispania
Reflection: We build on the works of others.

The sense of the holy is gained first from awareness that great events, especially the miraculous, have taken place in a particular location. The observance of tradition whether in the form of ancient liturgy or popular custom helps the pilgrim identify with ancient events ... These past wonders become appropriated by the pilgrim. The past becomes present. The pilgrim becomes one with all who have gone before.
Martin Robinson, *Sacred Places, Pilgrim Paths: An Anthology of Pilgrim*age, p.116.

The final years of Jacob bar Zebedee's life were spent in Jerusalem preaching among the Jews. Immediately following the death of Jesus,

---

[7] The work of Robert Eiseman, *James the Brother of Jesus*, maintains that James, the Greater, was completely fictitious and a product of narrative overlay to expunge from early Church writings the existence of Jesus' most powerful and influential sibling, James the Lesser. Eiseman believes that James, the Greater, was most probably the historical Theudas or Thaddaeus and synonymous with the apostles Thomas, Lebbaeus, Jude, the brother of James, Judas Iscariot and Simon Iscariot. Thaddaeus was beheaded in 45 AD during the reign of Herod of Chalcis (44 - 49), brother of Herod Agrippa I (37 - 44 AD) after the death of John, the Baptist. James, the Lesser (James, the Just, the Just One), first Head or Bishop of the Jerusalem Church and, thus, leader of the nascent Jewish / Christian Community or Ecclesia after the death of Jesus, was one of four siblings, all of whom were marginalized in the New Testament being made cousins, disciples or acquaintances of Jesus. "...These instances are all connected with the downplaying of the family of Jesus and writing it out of Scripture ... This was necessary because of the developing doctrine of the supernatural Christ and the stories about his miraculous birth." XVIII, James, the Brother of Jesus.) Eisenman concludes that the sons of Zebedee so frequently mentioned in the Gospels were also a literary device for obfuscation. James, the Just, and Thaddaeus were brothers and, thus, siblings of Jesus, and were in fact the sons of Zebedee so frequently mentioned in Scripture. (Eisenman, 924)

the leadership of the cult of Jesus fell to the original apostles. James the Lesser occupied a position of importance and power during those early years. Called by Mark *ho mikros*, "the runt", James the Lesser, bishop of the Jerusalem Church, co-headed the Council of Jerusalem in 50 AD and was among the original followers who evangelized outside of Judea. James, the Greater reportedly followed his lead and joined this first generation of missionaries. The nascent Christian community in the 40s, 50s, and the first several years of the 60s numbered only several thousand. The legendary history of Jacob's evangelism is reflected in the actual experiences of other apostles. Common to both versions was their hope to quickly convert the multitudes; a dream not easily realized.

Nevertheless, the spread of Christianity outside of Hispania increased dramatically by the year 100, almost four decades after the deaths of the original apostles. This largely an urban experience spread the Roman Empire from east to west across. Cities on the outer fringe of the empire in the occidental provinces such as Brittany and Hispania demonstrated a widespread resistance Christianization.

By the year 100, no Christian churches existed in Hispania. Cordova, the southern most urban settlement in Baetica, had the first recognized church by the year 200. Gades, the Phoenician port city on the southwest Atlantic coast, contemporary Cádiz, remained outside of Hispania's emerging Christian community until considerably after the third century. Few significant urban centers in the Iberian Peninsula had been Christianized before the beginning of the 4th century. A diverse non-Christian population would have proven to be very unreceptive to James, Paul or any of the other missionaries to Hispania. (Stark, *The Rise of Christianity*)

A North African origin of Spanish Christianity appears to be a more likely explanation for the spread of this new faith. The 7th Legion spearheaded a persecution, decreed by emperor Decio in 250 AD, dispersing segments of the small Christian enclaves in Baetica to the north and east. The character of certain documents from the early church particularly the canons of the Council of Elvira indicate a strong African influence, and thus may speak to this diaspora. Archaeological evidence for a thriving import economy based in northern Africa that used the markets of Gadir, Italica and Corduba exists as well. The remains of African-designed mosaics, ceramics, mausoleums and grave markers found in the south of Hispania underscore the intensity of this commerce. Lastly, the first chapels and churches show signs of Christian architectural components of African origin. (Stark)

The expansion of Christianity in Hispania appears to have moved from the south to the north. According to the Council of Elvira, the highest number of dioceses in the 4th century was situated in Baetica. However, smaller, less-numerous Christian enclaves existed in Zaragoza, León-Astorga and Mérida in the third century AD. Christianity in Hispania in the 300s was also decidedly urban, and began to penetrate the ranks of the Roman high society throughout the empire by the end of the 3rd century. (Stark)

Martyrdom was suffered by an increasing number of Christians in Hispania, their deaths postdating the executions of the major figures of the early church by almost two hundred years. Among the best know are Felix of Gerona, Justa and Rufina of Italica, and Justo and Pastor of Alcalá of Henares, Cucufate of Barcino and Emeterio and Celedonio of Calahorra. Nevertheless, before Christianity became a religious force in Hispania, an entire generation of apostles had already been executed. Jacob bar Zebedee, St. James the Greater, would be one of the first apostles to be martyred, dying in his native land of Judea.

Jacob's Martyrdom
Reflection: Not all paths end as we choose.

A pilgrim wanders through life, often limping, sometimes bewildered, at times quite lost; and the pilgrim is searching, often quite unconsciously, for something or someone to make sense of life, and certainly to make sense of death.
Basil Hume, *To Be a Pilgrim* (1984), p.38

Martyrdom at the request of the Sanhedrin and at the hands of the Roman State was a common end to the lives of many of the original followers of Jesus. Jacob bar Zebedee would share in this. His death is placed in the year 44 AD and preceded the devastating years of the 60s that witnessed the deaths of Paul and Peter. His execution followed that of St. Stephen who was executed in the winter of 36 - 37

AD. Early Church history sets the date of Jacob's execution on the 25th of March, marking his original feast day. Church authorities later commemorated his martyrdom on the July 25th. His death occurred at the hands of Herod Agrippa I, son of Aristolubus and grandson of Herod the Great, days before Passover. Agrippa ordered the beheading of Jacob bar Zebedee in the city of Jerusalem:

"Now at this time Herod the king set hands on certain members of the Church to persecute them. He killed James, the brother of John, with the sword." (Acts 12)

The apostle's body was left exposed to the elements outside the walls of the city as final punishment. His followers collected his remains at dusk and spirited his body and head out of the city to the coast. Herod Agrippa I would die in the spring of 44 AD before the completion of the third wall of Jerusalem. The *Brevarium Apostolorum,* which served as the basis for the *Sixth Age,* the 7th century work of Saint Julian of Toledo, indicates that the burial site of the martyred Jacob was located in Judea at *Cesarea* of Palestine, an arid region that extends between the delta of the River Nile and the Cirenaica. (Alarcón, *A la sombra de los templarios,* 331)

Jacob's early martyrdom preceded the executions of three major figures of the early Christian community; James the Lesser, Paul and Peter. Only St. Stephen, the first deacon of the Church of Jerusalem, was executed in the winter of 36-37 AD. James the Lesser, known as *the brother of the Lord*, was seized in the year 62 by Ananus. This new high priest brought James and other followers before the Sanhedrin, condemned them for breaking Jewish law, and ordered them stoned to death. Peter and Paul, who had spent significant periods away from Judea, suffered martyrdom in the 60's. Paul, arrested in the Temple of Jerusalem in 58, imprisoned in Caesarea Maritima, shipwrecked in Malta while awaiting word on his appeal to the Caesar, was finally transported to Rome where he was beheaded around 67 AD. Peter was the victim of the first officially sanctioned Roman persecution of the Christians by Emperor Nero. Christians were blamed for the burning of Rome in July of 64. Peter's death was recorded in Rome between the years 64 or 67 AD, suffering *crucifixion inversa.*

James' evangelistic accomplishments were meager. His mission to Roman Hispania might not have occurred, and his life ended earlier than his contemporaries. Yet, Jacob bar Zebedee passed into a legendary plane unequaled in scope and intensity of many of the other martyred apostles. His transformation into the figure of S*anto Iago*, patron saint of Spain, builds on a sparse historical reality and encompasses oral histories that blend his legendary exploits with pre-Christian mythic elements of northern Hispania. Ultimately, his legendary history echoes themes found in many world mythologies and links the stars of the Milky Way to the terrain of Galicia. We will gain greater insight into the origin of St. James's legendary history as well as the cultures that inhabited the Peninsula if we examine the myth and oral traditions that have come to be accepted as his actual biography.

Chapter 2
ST. JAMES IN THE WRITTEN RECORD

James and the *Legenda Sanctorum*
Reflection: Facts often hide among tales.

I do not see the road ahead of me.
I cannot know for certain where it will end.
Nor do I really know myself,
And the fact that I think I am following your will
Does not mean that I am actually doing so?
Thomas Merton (1915-1968), *A Prayer*

The historical Jacob bar Zebedee, martyred apostle from Judea, was renamed St. James the Greater, Spain's Santiago de Compostela, in medieval hagiographies and histories. Although popular accounts of Jacob's life referred to his being of the house of Zebedee, the historicity of the apostle's life, his religious background, and ties to the ascetic, Essene community succumbed to the growing corpus of legendary accounts which de-emphasized Jacob's Jewish heritage. The traditions referred to his legendary travels to Roman Hispania, spoke of James, the Greater or the Elder, and tied him to the emerging Christian traditions in Hispania. However, Jacob bar Zebedee, born in Judea, the martyred Essene Jew and cousin to Jesus, vanished from the historical record.

Accounts of St. James' missionary activity in Hispania derive from oral and written histories, the New Testament, and hagiographic narratives. The oldest and most-widely disseminated source, the *Legenda Sanctorum* commonly known as the *Golden Legend* of the 13th century Archbishop of Genoa, Jacobus de Voragine, bridges the historicity of the New Testament and the narrative of legend and folklore of the Middle Ages. The passages of this medieval hagiography chronicled Saint James' journeys through Gallaecia, his death in Judea, and his posthumous return to the Iberian Peninsula.

De Voragine, born between 1228 and 1230 in Varaggio on the Gulf coast of Genoa, became a Dominican friar, rose in the hierarchy of the Order of Preachers, and was appointed Archbishop of Genoa. He was recognized as a cleric of inexhaustible charity, and known as "the father of the poor." Author of numerous works among which was his commentary on Saint Augustine, the *Chronicle of Genoa*, Voragine is best remembered for his *Golden Legend*, a compendium of biographical information, popular lore, and widely accepted beliefs about the lives of the saints. Sherry Reames in *The Legenda Aurea: A Reexamination of Its Paradoxical History* indicates that this book's popularity of which over five hundred manuscript copies were made in a dozen languages, including High and Low German, Bohemian and Provencal, qualified it as a cultural and religious watershed. The *Legenda* is considered the second most frequently reproduced manuscript during the late Middle Ages, second only to the Bible.

The *Legenda Sanctorum, Readings on the Lives of the Saints,* explained the liturgical calendar's feasts and holidays and saints' days and included accounts of the saints' lives and their heroic actions. (Ryan and Ripperger, *The Golden Legend of Jacobus de Voragine*, Viii) This layman's lectionary chronicled the lives and works of the saints and provided ethical and moral instruction as well as inspiration to its readership. Although the *Legenda*, written between 1255 and 1266, compiled the popularly accepted lore of the saints' lives and martyrdoms, Church authorities questioned the accuracy of some of its renderings. Voragine clearly attempted to inspire and provide example for the general Christian audience. (Ryan and Ripperger, XII)

De Voragine's work places James in Spain for a brief period of ineffectual evangelization. Accompanied by nine followers, James journeys through the north of Spain and ends his wanderings in contemporary Zaragoza. The lectionary states that he left two of his nine followers in either Iria Flavia or Zaragoza and mentions the saint's return to Judea with the remaining seven, his exploits in Judea, and his martyrdom.

The sources for Voragine's commentaries about James' travels and evangelistic undertakings were based on Hugues, a Cluny abbot (1024-1109), Hugues de Saint-Victoria, a Parisian monk (1097-1141), Pope Calixto II (1119-1124?) and the work of the theologian, Jean Béleth, *Great History of Santiago,* written in the 12th century. Pope Leon XIII, who authenticated the relics in his papal bull Deus Ominpotens in 1884, further legitimized this literary tradition.

Travels and Travails
Reflection: His life's story is as complex as ours.

Good thoughts his onely friends,
His wealth a well-spent age,
The earth his sober Inne,
And quiet Pilgrimage.
Thomas Campion (1567-1620), *The Works of Thomas Campion*, ed. W Davies (1969), p. 43

The narratives of the legendary history of St. James' draw from many sources and vary in subtle ways. Yet, the versions share certain commonalities: a focus on his evangelistic activities and Marian visions in Hispania, his return to Jerusalem, the encounter with Hermogenes the magician, and the apostle's martyrdom. James, assigned to evangelize in Hispania, arrived at the Mediterranean coast of Roman *Baetica*, contemporary Andalucía and traveled through this province to Lusitania, known today as Portugal. He arrived and traveled through Gallaecia, Spain's Galicia, failing to convert the Austres. James fled from persecution at the hands of these local tribes and Roman soldiers, and journeyed to Caesar Augusta, the capital of the eastern province of the Tarraconensis, modern Zaragoza. During his travels the apostle had visions of Mary, the living mother of Jesus, in Iria Flavia and Caesar Augusta.

According to the most popular English version of the Golden Legend, translated by William Caxton in 1483, James "first preached in Judea and Samaria, and then went to Spain to sow the word of God." (*The Golden Legend*, 369) Popular lore claims that James departed Jerusalem seven years after Christ's death and arrived at the Mediterranean coast of the Roman province, *Baetica*, at either Carteia, located immediately east of Gibraltar, the port city of *Malaca*, Spain's Málaga or *Abdera*, the eastern terminus of the Roman road system. Tradition maintains that he passed through ancient Tartessos, the abandoned capital of the Tartessians.

These versions would indicate that a landing in Carteia would have been most likely, given that this settlement fell along the road south of Gades, the Phoenician mercantile center, and passed near Tartessos. The most direct route inland, however, headed from *Malaca* directly to the metropolis of *Hispalis* and its sister city, *Italica*, modern Sevilla. There is scant narrative on his travels to these two major urban centers of southern Hispania. *Hispalis* and *Carthago Nova*, contemporary Cartagena, in the southeastern Levante, were the major cities of the southern terminus of the occidental routes of the *Via Caesar Augusta*, a Roman highway system that criss-crossed the Peninsula. *Emérita Augusta*, contemporary Mérida, located northeast of the twin cities, *Hispalis* and *Italica*, provided an intermediary point for travelers in Roman Hispania. Merchants, soldiers, and every nature of traveler and pilgrim visited this major urban center and capital of Lusitania. James, the Greater, would have passed through *Emérita Augusta* on his way to the Atlantic coast.

The Romans attempted to conquer the Lusitanians shortly after the 3rd Punic War. In 151 BC a peace accord between the empire and Viriato, king of the Lusitanians, was violated when the Romans ambushed and slaughtered the tribe's cosignators. Almost 20 years later in 137 BC, a second and final agreement sealed the peace and opened this western section of the Peninsula to Roman mercantile expansion. James would have passed through these lands on his way to *Conimbriga*, the current river city of Coimbra, Portugal. Tradition does not account for his activities in this area, stating only that his journey turned north along the Atlantic highway up to *Bracara Augusta*, currently known as the Spanish town of Braga, then a border settlement near *Gallaecia*.

Popular lore and local histories indicate that the evangelistic activity of James intensified in the region of Iria Flavia. This early capital of the *Gallaecia* was located at either the contemporary Padrón, or at the current site of the city, Santiago de Compostela. Ambrosio de Morales cites local lore in his 16th century work, *Viaje santo,* and places the apostle in the hills of the Padrón Valley during the early years of his mission. James held mass at a spring associated with a local cult of water worship. Ambrosio states:

> "Climbing the mountain, half way up the slope, there is a church where they say that St. James prayed and held Mass and an abundant spring flows from under the main altar to the outside of the church, the coldest and most delicious I had seen in Galicia."

The narratives of the legend contend that the saint's prolonged stay in this region of Gallaecia proved to be unsuccessful. The tribal leaders reportedly rebuffed the saint's overtures and considered him to be an annoyance. His travels included visits to *Farum Brigantium*, the contemporary city of La Coruña, *Caronium*, located in the outskirts of current La Coruña, and *Munxía*, the Galician town of Muxía or Mugia located on the last stretches of the Finisterre along *the Muxia Way.*

James' Marian Visions
Reflection: Though unaccompanied, we never walk alone.

European pilgrimage is predominantly Marian. Christ's mother, Saint Mary, is the principal subject at nearly two-thirds of today's shrines.
Sidney and Mary Lee Nolan, *Christian Pilgrimage in Modern Western Europe,* (1989), p. 211

The ancient, Atlantic coastal settlement of Muxía provides the setting for James' first vision of Mary, the mother of Jesus. The living Mary reportedly appeared to the crestfallen James from a boat that approached the shore and miraculously transformed into stone. Mary's appearance revitalized and encouraged the apostle to continue his work among the locals. Lore mentions that at the site of this transformation, inhabited by Austres who populated the region east of the land of the Gallaecians, elongated sacrificial, stone altars commonly used for ritual sacrifice were found along the coast.

The accounts state that James spent seven years in this region. Though his evangelistic efforts met with little success, he did attract a following of local converts who reportedly numbered between two and nine. Many histories indicate that his two most faithful disciples, Atanasio and Theodore, would figure prominently in St. James' legendary history. Some histories maintain that the apostle and his two disciples stayed in Hispania, one heading the bishopric of Zaragoza. Other sources indicate that they accompanied the apostle's body from Judea back to Galicia and were buried alongside their master upon their deaths.

His journey through the north would certainly have taken him through the provincial capital, *Lucus Augusta*, contemporary Lugo. James would have visited the Celt Iberian cities of north central Hispania, preaching to the Romans, Celts and Celt Iberians of this region. The legendary accounts depict the saint during his initial years as a lone missionary, staff in hand, accompanied by a dog who befriended the saint errant in the region of the *Legion VII Gémina*. The cities of *Clunia* and *Osma* and the former Celt Iberian stronghold, *Numantia* stood along James' route. He would have finished his journey at the crossroads of *Caesaraugusta*, contemporary Zaragoza. Regardless of the source, all of the narrations of his travels in Gallaecia underscore the evangelistic disappointments of James. Apparitions and occasional miracles failed to improve the apostle's efforts.

Dejected and desirous of the comforts of Jerusalem, James was buoyed by his second vision of Mary. According to popular history, Mary appeared to the apostle on the banks of the Ebro River in the year 40 AD. She encouraged him not to lose faith and instructed him to build a chapel in her honor. Isabel Allardyce in her wonderful compilation of church lore and history, *Historic Shrines of Spain*, narrates the exchange:

> "My son James, the Most High and Mighty God of Heaven has chosen this place that you may consecrate and dedicate here a temple and house of prayer where, under the invocation of my

name. He wishes to be adored and served." (Allardyce, *Historic Shrines of Spain*, 8)

In another account of this vision, Mary appeared to him shortly after James disembarked at the mouth of the Ebro River. After traveling upriver with seven disciples, James fell asleep in the woods and awoke to the sight of angels descending among flashes of light. The Virgin appeared and either alighted upon a column of stone or placed a wooden or stone statuette of her likeness on a column of jasper. She requested that James build a chapel to house this *Virgen del Pilar, Virgin of the Pillar.*[8] Allardyce cites the instructions Mary gave St. James:

"The Pilar will remain here, and upon it my image which in this place where you will build my temple will last and endure with the Holy Faith until the end of the world." (Allardyce, 9)

James oversaw the construction of a chapel and, in the precincts of this small temple, enshrined the stone on which Mary stood. Legend maintains that this was reportedly the first church built by an apostle in honor of the mother of Jesus. Local Church lore indicates that James upon completion of the project named Athanasius its first bishop and ordained Theodore, its first priest. The basilica *Nuestra Señora del Pilar of Zaragoza* stands on this site today.

Although further accounts of the journeys of James in Hispania place him in many other locales, the Marian visions are their unifying themes. James became closely associated with images and statues of Mary during his last years in the Iberian Peninsula. Several accounts state that he distributed statuettes of the Virgin along the northern route of the Roman highway in Hispania. The wood or stone icons he, by some accounts, brought from Jerusalem or fashioned by hand. This region

---

[8] A 40 cm.-tall, black virgin statue is currently housed in the Cathedral of Nuestra Señora del Pilar whose feast day is celebrated on the 12th of October.

of Spain reportedly has the highest incidence of black virgin statues and reliquaries.[9] Zaragoza with its Virgen del Pilar also known as the *Madonna del Pilar,* one of the most popular black virgins of the Iberian Peninsula, is the premier Marian sanctuary of Spain.[10] Many of the accounts states that the saint traveled with two younger disciples, maintaining a sacred triad found earlier between Jesus, James, the Greater and his younger brother, John. One variant legend numbers James' disciples as seven. *The Golden Legend* indicates that there were ultimately nine disciples, two of whom remained in Spain to continue the saint's work. According to some accounts these disciples faithfully followed James and were his only evangelistic successes in the Peninsula.

James' port of entry into the Peninsula varies as well; some stories claiming entrance through the Ulla River in Galicia, others indicating arrival at Tarragona at the mouth of the Ebro River. All of these accounts end with a period of unsuccessful evangelism and his return to Jerusalem.

Magic, Conversion and Death by the Sword
Reflection: Life asks change and sacrifice of us.

The idea of pilgrimage is much older than Christianity ... involves discomfort and hardship ... where the meaning of existence, of the seemingly arbitrary nature of current happenings, will become clear; where there is justice, peace and love.
Margaret Pawley, *Prayers for Pilgrims,* (1991), p. xiii

Upon James' return to Jerusalem, he encountered the magician Hermogenes. Triumph over magic, conversion, and martyrdom appear in the final accounts of the apostle's life. *The Golden Legend* provides a detailed rendering of James' activities upon his return to Judea from Spain. However, biblical references concerning the actions of James, the Greater, are scarce. The work *Great History of James* by Jean Béleth provides detailed accounts of his final years

[9] The Black Virgin statues and their accompanying cults descend from the ancient Mother Goddess beliefs of early man, and the Babylonian, Sumerian and Canaanite traditions of the Great Mother Goddess. (Begg, *The Cult of the Black Virgin*)
[10] The Madonna del Pilar .The legends surrounding the Madonna del Pilar claim that the stone from which the statue is fashioned fell from the stars over 2,000 years ago. (Munro, *On Glory Roads*)

in Jerusalem. James' encounter with the magician Hermogenes and his martyrdom figure prominently in all of the available narratives. Abdias in his histories of the apostles dating from the 4th century provides details for his final activities as well. (4:1-9)

Hermogenes, a renowned magician, and his companion, Philetus, challenged the veracity of the teachings James espoused. Philetus, as ordered by his magician master, confronted James and his disciples, asking the saint to deny the authenticity of the miraculous works of Jesus and his apostles. Philetus intended to denounce James before the Jews. The saint reasoned with his accuser, performed certain miracles in the name of the Savior, and converted the magician's emissary.

Philetus returned to Hermogenes and denounced the pagan's magic. Hermogenes cast a spell on his former disciple, immobilizing him with incantations. James became aware of his new disciple's fate and sent an emissary with a blessed cloak or "kerchief" to break the spell. The saint instructed the bearer of the garment to have Philetus say, "God raises those who have fallen. He frees those who are imprisoned."

The Golden Legend provides a similar verse which parallels the Béleth account, "The Lord lifts up them that fall, and looses the captives." (*Golden Legend*, 370) Upon receiving the cloak and uttering the acclamation, Philetus was freed and fled to James.

Hermogenes, infuriated with the success of his rival, sent demons to capture and return Philctus and apprehend the apostle. Béleth recounts the use of a magic cloak that ensnared the evil spirits, sending them in pursuit of the pagan magician. *The Golden Legend* claims that the spirits were held back from the saint by burning chains fashioned by God. In both cases, the evil spirits were tamed and sent to ensnare the magician. Hermogenes, captured by his own creation, was bound and delivered to James. The prisoner repented, converted to Christianity, and sought protection from the vengeful spirits. James provided him with his walking stick as a safeguard. Hermogenes offered to burn his many volumes of magical incantations. James, wary of the evil, which might have been released by the bonfires, instructed his new disciple to throw the books into the sea.

James' success angered the Abiathar, High Priest of the Sanhedrin, who encouraged his followers to apprehend James, the Greater, and deliver him to Herod Agrippa I. The king condemns him to death. Acts 12:2 recount briefly his decision:

"It was about this time that King Herod started persecuting certain members of the Church. He beheaded James the brother of John and when he saw that this pleased the Jews, he decided to arrest Peter as well. This was during the days of Unleavened Bread ..."

Both versions indicate that James encountered a paralytic on route to the executioner's block and cured him saying, "In the name of Jesus Christ, for whom I am being led to die, be thou made whole and arise and bless thy Creator." Josias, the scribe who led the saint by a rope tied around his throat, converted, refused to denounce his newly acquired faith, and suffered martyrdom with James. Shortly before their execution, James baptized the scribe and was decapitated forthwith on March 25th in the year 44 AD. The Golden Legend notes the change of the date of the feast day to the 25th of July which reportedly coincided with the transport of the saint's remains to Compostela from Iria Flavia. Upon his execution, James the Greater began his journey into the realm of myth and legend and would forever change the cosmology of Christian Spain.

Textual Support for St. James' in Hispania
Reflection: We may come to know truth through others.

The peregrinus is the foreigner, walking over the land of others, seeking the Other.
Anne Dumoulin, "Towards a Psychological Understanding of the Pilgrim', Lumen Vitae 32, (1997): 112-3

The appearance and dissemination of the accounts of James's evangelization of Hispania occur outside of Spain in the 6th and 7th centuries. Record of the saint's activities appears in *Apostolic Catalogues* written in Greek in the 500s. The *Brevarium Apostolorum* mentions James and his evangelistic efforts in Hispania and circulates throughout Western Europe in the 7th century. A history of the early martyrs, compiled by Adon in France around 860, mentions the saint's presence and travels in the Iberian Peninsula as well as his shrine at Compostela. An English abbot of the 8th century from Mamesbury writes the first British work, *Primitus Hispanias convertit dogmate gentes,* establishing James, the Greater, as a participant in the evangelistic effort in the Iberian Peninsula.

No significant theological work confirms the saint's presence until the resurfacing of the *Brevarium* in the late 8th century. Beato of Liébana in his *Commentaries on the Apocalypse* amended the contents of the *Brevarium* indicating that James had evangelized and was *buried* in Hispania.[11] This Asturian prelate becomes the foremost promoter of the St. James presence in Hispania. He writes hymns for King Mauregato in 783 and 788 that implore James's intercession and extol his saintly qualities. In the 9th century, Notker from the monastery of St. Gall in Switzerland refers to James's presence in Hispania. The works of Florus de Lyon, 806 - 838, present a history of martyrs and mentions St. James' relics in Iria Flavia.

Notwithstanding the theological polemics and initial absence of archival evidence as well as local traditions' contradictory nature, several histories, popular legends, and written accounts maintain that James traveled the north of Hispania, crossing northeastern Luisitania, Galatia and Tarraconesis, contemporary Leon, Galicia and Aragón.[12] Popular accounts state that he entered Hispania from the south, contemporary Andalucía or the Roman *Baetica* and traveled northwest through Coimbra and Braga to the province of Gallaecia. Arriving at Iria Flavia, later known as Padrón, he preached in Muxía located on the narrow isthmus near the cliffs of Finisterre. At the end of his wanderings, James proved unsuccessful in his efforts at converting the pagan populations of northern Hispania.

After four years of fruitless evangelizing in Hispania, the legendary St. James the Greater returned to Judea joining a small

---

[11] The presence of relics associated with St. James may find its genesis in the early years of the Muslim invasion of the Peninsula. It is believed that members of the Christian community of Emerita Augusta may have journeyed to Gallaecia with the relics of several saints including those of St. James in the early 8th century. Fleeing the advancing Muslim armies of Muza in 712 the faithful transported the relics to Galicia where they founded the church of Santa María, later rededicated to St. James. Archaeological evidence of a church dedicated to Saint Maria has been found which reportedly contained the relics of the True Cross, Saint John, the Baptist, Saints Peter and Paul and those of the brothers Zebedee

[12] In the Semitic languages of Hebrew or Aramaic this could have meant relative

enclave of Christians led by James, the Lesser, known as the *brother* of Jesus. Popular legend melds with archival Church history and locates James in Jerusalem with the nascent Christian community of the 30s. His execution ordered by Herod Agrippa would occur in 44 AD.

Chapter 3
ST. JAMES RETURNS TO HISPANIA

The Voyage Home
Reflection: May our journeys not own us, but steer us home.

Sometimes we shall feel that we have lost sight of the track, like travelers in the Sahara when a sandstorm has blotted out the route. But we yearn to keep on, regardless of feeling, afraid or uncertain or perplexed.
Olive Wyon, *The Way of the Pilgrim,* (1958), pp. 124-5

The death of the apostle, the recovery of his remains, and their return to Spain combine the historic with the legendary. The *Golden Legend* references Béleth's narrative that described the removal of St. James' body and its subsequent journey to Spain. Unnamed disciples transported the body to the coast and stored it in a rudderless boat without steersman. They set sail "trusting to Providence."

Other popular versions recounted that two disciples, Atanasio and Theodore, collected the apostle's remains at sundown. Herod Agrippa I had prohibited their burial and ordered that the body be dumped outside the precincts of the city, exposed as carrion for wild dogs. The apostle's friends and followers loaded his remains on a crewless ship that they found on the coast provisioned for a long-distance voyage. Atanasio and Theodore set sail guided by invisible angels.

The identity of these two disciples is not consistent. Some descriptions maintain that the recently converted magician, Hermogenes, and his assistant spirited the body away, magically transporting it to *Gallaecia*. However, most versions highlight the role of Atanasio and Theodore in the retrieval of the apostle's body; disciples of the original group of seven that returned with James from Hispania.

The ship with its mystical cargo sailed out onto the Mediterranean, through the Pillars of Hercules, along the Atlantic coast of Lusitania, and entered the *ría* Noela, one of the many estuaries along the coast of Gallaecia. The duration of the voyage remains unclear, lasting either seven days or one solitary night. A variant version of the voyage involves a crew of seven angels; absent the two disciples. Nevertheless, the destination remains unchanged as well as the route.

The oral legends and early written accounts indicate that the ship came to ground in the land of the Austres, descendants of the Celtic tribes that inhabited the north west of *Hispania*. Divergent oral traditions name their point of disembarkation as either Iria Flavia or Iris Flavia, a Roman settlement, flanked by the Ulla and Tambre rivers and located at the terminus of the ria Noela. Pacified and settled by the soldiers of the VII Gemina Legion and Hispano-Romano peoples, this site rested in the fertile valley of D'Amaía. Iria Flavia has been identified as one of the early capitals of Roman *Gallaetia Braccarensis*.

Liquid Stone and Scallop Shells
Reflection: Substance is not eternal.

"The soul that is attached to anything however much good there may be in it, will not arrive at the liberty of divine union. For whether it be a strong wire rope or a slender and delicate thread that holds the bird, it matters not, if it really holds it fast; for, until the cord be broken the bird cannot fly."
St. John of the Cross

The disposition and transport of the body of James initiate a series of magico-religious narratives. The disciples, Atanasio and Theodore, unloaded the remains of the saint, placing them on an *arca solis* or pagan sacrificial altar at the shore. The stone began to liquefy and fit the contours of the remains, forming a perfect sarcophagus for the saint.[13] Variant forms of the legend indicate that angels loaded the form-fitting lapidary onboard in Joppa. Other accounts state that the stone assumed a molten state as the boat rounded the Pillars of Hercules. Another maintains that upon entering the waters of the Forbidden Sea, the Atlantic, a perfect stone coffin formed around the saint's remains. These accounts echo the mythic appearance of Osiris who drifted ashore in a burial chest. The wood of the tamarisk tree protectively encased Osiris, the Egyptian king of eternity and the Ruler of Everlastingness.[14] But it is stone that envelops the body of St. James, one of the *sons of Thunder,* and ushers him to his final resting place.

The first miraculous event associated with the saint's remains occurred on the Galician seashore during a wedding celebration. A horseman and his ride fell into the sea reappearing from beneath the waves inexplicably unharmed. Encrusted around the horse's mane and the rider's garments were scallop shells; St. James' symbol to be worn by future pilgrims along his *Way.*

The scallop shell harkens back to the fertility symbols used in the genesis stories of Aphrodite and Venus, who begotten from divine spermatozoa, emerged from scallop shells. These seashells characteristically have been found in Paleolithic burials sites, believed to have been placed on the eyes of the deceased or left as burial

---

[13] The alchemical-like transmutation of stone from solid to liquid to solid figured in both versions of Santiago's return. The transmutation narrative sparked the interest of alchemists and physicians alike who considered Santiago to be their patron saint and the route to the tomb St. Iago the earthly projection of the Milky Way and the symbol of the Mercurial Work. Alexander Roob in his *Hermetic Museum: Alchemy and Mysticism,* quotes a German hymn from 1553, "Narrow and slippery is the way surrounded by water and fire." The transmutation of stone to liquid to stone and wood to stone is a common theme in the St. James histories. The ship which transported Mary, the mother of Jesus, to the Atlantic shore during St. James' first Marian vision changed to stone as it approached the beach and the venue for Mary's second appearance in Zaragoza is on top of a stone column. An accounting of James' travels through the north of Hispania maintains that he fashioned and distributed black stone (possibly dark wood) statues of the Virgin. (Roob, 700)

[14] Arthur Cotterell relates the appearance of a coffer in which Seth, his brother, and his fellow conspirators entrapped Osiris. The coffer coming to rest at the foot of a tamarisk tree at Byblos, in Phoenicia, grows around it and encloses it within its trunk. (*The MacMillan Illustrated Encyclopedia of Myths and Legends,* 145)

ornaments. Pre-Christian graves found in the vicinity of the *Way* also contained these shells. Imbued with a life-giving, mystical quality, pulverized *St. James Scallop shells* were sold as an aphrodisiac during the Middle Ages. Alchemists embraced St. James as their patron and his shell-symbol as their own. [15]

Encounters with the Queen of Wolves
Reflection: Not all will receive you with open arms.

God of the nomad and the pilgrim ...May our doors be open to guests and our hearts to one another and so all our traveling is lighter and together we reach the goal.
Mary Batchelor, ed., *The Lion Prayer Collection,* (1992), p. 139

Varying accounts of the transport of the apostle's body figured in narratives that highlighted the persona of Loba, the Queen of the Wolves. Although there is significant divergence on the actual transport of the saint's remains, the narratives concur on the adventures of the disciples and the local personages whom they encountered. Some versions note that angels levitated the stone to a nearby mountain for burial. In others the disciples drive a cart pulled by bulls or oxen that transport James' remains to a promontory. Still in some versions soldiers of a local Austre queen accompany the stone-encased body to a mountain site and respectfully cover it with stones. All of the accounts locate the burial site in an elevated location, known either as *Pico Sacro*, Sacred Peak or a site associated with a marble sarcophagus, *Arca Marmónica.* All of these versions detail the movement of the body east and inland from its point of disembarkation. The burial of the remains occurs on a mountain, a promontory or a hillock.

---

[15] In hermetic symbolism the coquille St. Jacques, the scallop shell of Santiago, represents the principle of Mercury know as the "traveler" or "pilgrim" and must be worn by those who wish to obtain the star, and realize the Mercurial work, product of the Philosopher's Stone. Hermetic pilgrims traveled to Compostela with the hopes of acquiring Jewish and Arab hermetic secrets from foreign mystics making pilgrimage to see Santiago from the south of Spain. Nicolas Flamel, alchemist of the early 1400's, stated, "That is the point at which all alchemists must begin. With their pilgrim's staff as a guide and the scallop as a sign, they must undertake this long and dangerous journey, half on water (liquid) and half on land (solid) first as pilgrims, then as pilots." (Roob, 701)

The following is a synopsis of one of the most frequently cited versions of the exploits of Atanasio and Theodore. Upon heading inland the disciples encounter a powerful Austre queen, *Loba* or *Lupa, Queen of Wolves,* and relate to her the miraculous happenings associated with their master.[16] Impressed with the powers of the Christian holy man, she orders that her soldiers retrieve the remains of the saint and bring them to her palace. Soon afterwards the queen, uneasy with the foreigners and fearful of their magic, requests that they leave and seek an audience with Régulo, *the High Priest of the Ara Solis.*

Régulo resided in Duyo and is portrayed as an adversary of the disciples. Several traditions call him a powerful, Christian-hating magician who imprisoned Atanasio and Theodore. Some descriptions claim that Régulo was a Roman garrison commander; others indicate that he was a king or noble. Some narrations identify the disciples' persecutor as the Roman Legate Filotro who lived in Dugium near Finisterre.

The imprisonment of the two disciples occasions the second miracle associated with St. James. Mysterious lights appeared inside the disciples' cell, outlining an invisible door to freedom. This miraculous escape enraged Régulo who sent his troops after the fleeing disciples. The third miracle manifests when the bridge over the river Tambre or Támara collapsed killing the disciples' pursuers. *The Golden Legend* states:

"The king sent soldiers in pursuit of them; but just as these soldiers were crossing a bridge, the bridge collapsed and the soldiers were drowned. At these points the king feared for himself and his people, and repented."

The symbolism of this divine intervention and the disciples' triumphant escape from pagan Rome would hardly have escaped the readership of the *Golden Legend.* The similarity between James' encounter with the magician, Hermogenes, in Judea and the evil Régulo may give insight into the intent of the writers of James' legendary history. The accounts that portrayed Régulo as a Roman

---

[16] Some accounts identify Lupa as a pagan woman of high standing in the fortified settlement of Lupario.

official, the collapsing bridge and the demise of the pursuers of the disciples underscore early Christianity's triumph over Imperial Rome.

Atanasio and Theodore returned to the Austre queen, requesting that she provide them with a cart and bulls to transport the body. She complied by sending them on a journey to Mount Illianus where the royal oxen were kept. Along the way the disciples encountered a fire-breathing dragon. The disciples "held a cross to him and he was cloven asunder." (*Golden Legend*, 370) The beast, a symbol of unleashed Nature, disintegrated when shown the cross.[17]

When the disciples reached the royal pasture, they discovered that the oxen were ferocious bulls that charged them. The cross of Christ held on high tamed the wild animals. The bull, symbol of the fertility cults in the Peninsula, succumbs to Christian symbology. His disciples "made the sign of the cross over the bulls and they became as meek as lambs."(373) Hitched to the cart and without guidance from the disciples, the docile bulls pulled the lapidary containing the remains of the saint directly to the palace of the queen. Astonished by the disciples' tenacity and the saint's powers, Queen Loba converted to Christianity and offered her palace as a burial place for James.

Once set free, the bulls climbed a promontory and wandered to a clearing where they intuitively pawed the ground, unearthing a spring. A small chapel dedicated to the apostle commemorates the discovery of the spring and stands close to the fountain, *Fonseca* or *Fuente Seca*. The disciples let providence guide the animals to the saint's final resting place on an elevated field. The saint's burial enclosure was built on this site and his remains entombed there.

[17] The dragon is derived from the Mesopotamian chaos-dragon and is another example of the integrative nature of the St. James legendary history.

An Uncertain Tomb
Reflection: Stone may not mark our final resting place.

*I had been disappointed at first at the noisy ending to the pilgrimage, but as I
sat, I became glad that is was this way. We need temples, churches and shrines,
we need solitude and silence, but we need all these things to make us more
aware of the mystery in which we are all living all the time.*
Howard Hughes, *Walk to Jerusalem,* (1991), p.239

Hillocks, star fields, and numerous oral history combine to establish the final resting place of the apostle. Some accounts maintain that the body was removed to a nearby settlement known as *Liberum Donum (Domum)* or *Libre-don,* a site located in a clearing which later became Compostela. The saint's tomb was known as the *arca marmónica,* marble tomb. Considered an ancient burial place during the Roman epoch, today it is called the hill of San Fiz de Solovio. The hilly field would come to be known as the Field of Stars, Campo de las Estrellas. The site was located along the Celtic route dedicated to the constellation *Can Major* or the *Rainbow of Lug,* god of light. [18]

After the burial of the apostle, the Austre queen reappeared in his legendary history, offering to destroy the pagan temple of the *Arca Solis.* The disciples declined her offer, departed her mountain palace, which they named *Pico Sacro,* Sacred Mount, and began to evangelize in pagan settlements throughout northern Hispania. Various accounts number the followers as nine. In numerous versions, the two original disciples, Theodore (*Theodosius*) and Atanasio (*Anastasius*) remained to guard the tomb. The remaining seven pursued their missionary activities throughout the Peninsula. Other accounts maintain that Theodore guarded the tomb and Atanasio remained in Zaragoza as its archbishop. The most popular and frequently written history has these two faithful disciples as the caretakers of the apostle's tomb. Upon their deaths, they were buried next to their master. The seven remaining disciples returned to Jerusalem. This version maintains the sacred triad, comprised of a master and his two acolytes. The spiritually charged number seven also reappears in several of the

[18] James Campell indicates Lug's association with the night sky. Arthur Cotterell associates Lugh with the sun. Variant forms of his name (Welsh Lleu, Gaelic Lugos) indicate an affiliation of the name with the Galician city, Lugo. Light, nocturnal or solar, is clearly associated with this divinity.

versions, maintaining the legendary history's link to the night skies and ancient mythology.

Early Christians of Hispania reportedly visited the burial site near Iria Flavia, venerating the relics of Santiago and his faithful disciples. The Christian community that developed near the burial site suffered persecution at the hands of the Romans in the third century AD and was dispersed several decades after the apostle's interment. The pilgrimage tradition was abandoned and Santiago's burial place was lost in history. (Starkie, 16-23) The memory of the shrine was forgotten for over six hundred years until its rediscovery in the early ninth century. Its discovery began the final stage of the narrative of the St. James legendary history; the revelation of the tomb and the early pilgrimage to the saint's burial site.

Chapter 4
STARS REVEAL THE TOMB AND PILGRIMAGE BEGINS

The Discovery of the Tomb
Reflection: Revelation comes from not one, but many mouths.

It seemed impossible to realize that we were on this holy ground at last; we moved on in silence, the speaking silence of a dream.
A. Mary Dobson, *Mount Sinai,* 1925, pp. 34-5

Astral events, heavenly music, and an oak tree led to the discovery of the ancient tomb and initiated the final stage of the St. James legendary history. These accounts begin with the discovery of the crypt in the early 9th century. An ascetic hermit known as Pelayo (identified also as Pelagio or Pelagius) discovered the burial site. Told in a vision that God would reveal the location of the apostle, Pelayo noticed bright lights hovering over a thicket of oak trees on a hilltop. Angels and music accompanied the sighting. Some versions indicate that Pelayo as well as other shepherds and hermits witnessed the lights and heard celestial music over the cluster of bushes and woods.

In other accounts, Pelayo, depicted as a simple shepherd, discovered a flickering star that appeared over a forest of oaks, marking the site of the tomb. This hermit shepherd who fed himself on honey and grasses[19] reportedly saw either a shower of falling stars or dancing lights over a solitary oak tree or a grove of oak trees on a rise in an open field which bore the name *Amaea* or *Amaí*.[20] Celestial music accompanied the vision. Not dissimilar to the star of Bethlehem, St. James' astral phenomenon led his discoverer to a terrestrial site where a sacred personage awaited. An astral event, which figured in the revelation of the Christ child, and the Druidic symbol, the oak tree, found union in the discovery of the apostle's tomb. This intertwining of an ancient pre-Christian religion and the Church's corpus of beliefs provided the footing for the initial stages of the legendary history of St. James.

Other Christian residents of San Fiz de Solovio saw and reported the extra normal occurrence to the local bishop, Teodomiro. The bishop whose episcopal seat was in Iria Flavia, located 17 kilometers from the discovery site, ordered a three-day fast before proceeding to the location. The search party, led by Pelayo and overseen by Theodomir, discovered a Roman mausoleum built over a crypt whose marble sarcophagus contained the remains of three individuals. The most widely circulated account maintains that a plaque, which was found at the burial site, claimed that the remains were those of St. James the Greater. The tomb's location was recorded as being at a site called *Marmaric* or *Arcis Marmoricis*, between the rivers Sur and Timbre in the district of Amaia in the diocese of Iria.

Accounts vary at this point. Some indicate that a stone altar and graves of three separate skeletons, one decapitated, were found. Others state that a marble sepulcrum was encountered. Dated to the Roman period by sundry artifacts found on site, the crypt contained the remains of an individual who was determined to be Saint James, the Greater. The bishop traveled to Oviedo, the capital of the Asturian kingdom, and reported the discovery to the king,

---

[19] The similarity between John, the Baptist and the hermit discoverer of James' tomb are poignant. Eleanor Munro comments on the similarity between the precursor to Jesus and this hermit who prayed for deliverance from the Moor and saw the star that led him to the location of St. James' crypt. (Eleanor Munro, *On Glory's Paths*, 189)

[20] The earliest reporting of the existence of a belief in St. James of Compostela appears in a French Apostolic Catalogue written by Adón in the 11th century. Reports of the discovery of a tomb in the valley of Amaea date from 830 B.C. and cited in *Santiago en Galicia* written by Luis Maria Duchense, 1900.

Alfonso II, the Chaste. He in turn presented the case to Pope Leo III and Charlemagne, the Emperor. Pilgrimage began soon after the announcement of the find.

Alfonso II announced his plans to build a modest church at this site. (Starkie, 22–24) Alfonso II communicated the news of the discovery to Pope León III who in turn informed Charlemane, Emperor of the Holy Roman Empire. Afonso II made pilgrimage to the site and ordered the construction of three churches. The one dedicated to James, the Greater was built in 820. Decades later this original structure would be demolished and a larger structure built by Alfonso III with the help of Bishop Sisnando. (Américo Castro, *España en su Historia*) Compostela with its temple dedicated to the apostle would become the episcopal seat by the end of the 11th century.

Charlemagne would enter the corpus of the St. James legendary narrative, lending further legitimacy to the nascent cult. Legend maintains that Charlemagne, after decisively defeating the Saracens, answered a celestial voice which called to him from the Milky Way saying:

"This is the path of St. James and I am that Apostle. My body is in Galicia, but no man knoweth where and Saracens oppress the land. The starry way signifies that you shall go at the head of a host, and after you, people on pilgrimage until the end of time."

Accounts maintain that the emperor followed the star field to Compostela in 814, a year before his death and donated the booty from his latest campaign to the construction of the city's churches. After arriving at the site, the emperor paid homage to the apostle and continued to the Atlantic coast. A mystery boat appeared to Charlemagne, reportedly the very same craft that carried St. James from Joppa. The emperor walked on the water and boarded the boat which took him out to sea where he threw a spear into the abyss of the Atlantic Ocean. Though the emperor's visit to Galicia was fictitious, these widely circulated accounts made public his recognition of the crypt and its relics as well as his approval of pilgrimage to the shrine.

The discovery of the crypt appears not to have been widely documented in Asturian archives at the time of Charlemagne's coronation in 800. However, French religious historians of the late 9th century produced several written descriptions of St. James the Greater. These histories of the saint's life familiarized the faithful with the existence and location of the apostle's relics, and the miraculous interventions associated with them. Starkie refers to V. de Praga who in turn cited the work, the *Martyrdom of Adon* written before 860 which announced the discovery of the tomb and the relics of the apostle. (Praga, *Historia Peregrinaciones a Santiago*, Madrid, 1948, Volume I, 34)

The small church built by Alfonso II would become an internationally recognized site of Christian pilgrimage by the middle of the 9th century. The Arab poet Yahya ben Alhacam, known popularly as *Algacél*, native of Jaén and contemporary of Alfonso III, commented in 845 on the steady flow of pilgrims to the site:

> "Their Kaaba is a colossal idol that is located in the center of the church. They swear allegiance to it and many come from distant lands, even from Rome, believing that the tomb is that of one of the twelve apostles, the most beloved of Isa, or Jesus. Blessings and the good news of God descend upon him and over our Prophet ..." (Alarcón, 38)

An upsurge in pilgrimage occurred after St. James interceded and aided in the defeat of the Muslim forces at Clavijo in 844. St. James the Greater's reported participation in this pivotal military event not only inextricably linked him to the nascent Spanish unity of the 9th century, but significantly increased pilgrimage to his tomb. Due to the heavy volume of pilgrims which could not be accommodated in the small church, Alfonso III, the Great ordered its demolition and the construction of a *cathedra* to house the shrine. The bishop's new seat and enclosure of the relics was completed in 872 and consecrated in 899. Almanzor considered the "anti-Christ" by 10th century millenarians would raze this structure in 997.

The Scimitar Conquers Spain
Reflection: Adversity lasts less than its memory.

"The Moor ... rings out the Tocsin bell ...
Now, God and Saint Iago strike, for the good cause of Spain!
By Heaven, the Moors prevail! The Christians yield!
Their coward leader ... mounts to quit the field."
Sir Walter Scott, The Vision of Don Roderick: XIX-XXI, 1811.

The 8th and 9th centuries were dire years for the fledgling Christian communities of northern Spain. The Arab-Berber invasion of 711 vanquished the Visigoth armies in less than a decade. Muslim hegemony in the Iberian Peninsula encountered few significant challenges. The Christians of the Cantabrian Mountain region were the exception. By the 9th century, Christian Spain had been reduced to a narrow northern strip, which ran from the Mediterranean coastal city of Barcelona in the Spanish March through Navarra into the mountains of the kingdom of Asturias, terminating in Galicia. A bulbous shaped, no-man's-land extruded north of Muslim Salamanca, and ran the length of the River Duero, past the contemporary Portuguese-Spanish border, bisected by the River Arlanzón, and included the cities of Burgos and León.

Popular accounts maintain that the Christian mountaineers in the caves of Covadonga began the Reconquest in 722. The Asturian and Cantabrian guerrilla fighters led by the chieftain, Pelayo, held off Muslim forces from their mountain stronghold, signaling the beginning of the Christian resistance to the Muslim advances to the north. Charles Martel turned back the Muslim push through southern France in 732 at Poitiers. The Christians consolidated their holdings by establishing the first kingdom of Asturias with its capital in Oviedo in 791.

Christian hegemony over the northwest was tenuous. The Muslim forces of Hisam I destroyed the new capital in 794. The following year the Asturian armies suffered defeats in Babia, Quirós, Nalón and the rebuilt Oviedo, which had been rebuilt from an earlier Muslim incursion, was sacked again. However, Muslim military prowess was compromised on occasion. Alfonso II managed to conquer Lisbon, defeated the Moors in Pancorbo in 816, and retook Nalón in 825.

Christian-held territory began to move south, as the acquisition of Muslim lands and the repopulation of territories outside of the protection of the Cantabrian Mountains became a reality. A constantly changing frontier, raids and pitched battles, and brief periods of peace characterized this period of national solidification. At the same time, intrigues among the Christian royalty complicated control of the newly conquered lands. King Mauregato, who reined 783 to 788, bastard son of Alfonso I, usurped the throne of Alfonso II and imprisoned his father's wife, Queen Adosinda. Alfonso II, patron of James, the Greater, regained the throne only after the death of Mauregato.

Not withstanding the frequent infighting among Christian kingdoms, the dynamic of the Reconquest was clear; Muslims and Christians fought to establish military, cultural, and religious hegemony. Nevertheless, the act of conquest in Spain was not based on obliteration, but rather assimilation. Intermarriage, conversions, either forced or willing, and the occasional ecclesiastical détente, linguistic borrowings, and culinary exchanges occurred along the shifting boundary between Moor and Christian. Each observed his opponent's military tactics, learned the other's language, and shared monotheistic beliefs founded in the Holy Land, venerating sages, prophets, and saintly persons.

The zealotry of the Muslim faith fused militancy and religiosity. The message of Islam, manifested in the teachings of Mohammed, the sacred writings of the Koran, and the concept of holy war, *jihad*, united the disparate tribes and peoples of Islam. On the other hand, regional loyalties and political infighting divided the Christians in post-Roman Visigoth Spain. The Suevi of the northwest, the Visigoths, Basques, Franks, and Vandals formed a conflictive religious and cultural patchwork across the Peninsula. The Visigoth populations who brought their Arian doctrine across the Pyrenees lacked common cultural and religious cause with the Hispano Romano and Jewish populations on the eve of the Arabic invasion of 711. Upon the conversion of Recared in 587, the Visigoth throne seated in Toledo began the persecution of Hispania's Jewish population, estimated to be over one million subjects. After the failed revolt of the Jews in 694 and successive coups, conspiracies, and intrigues among the Christian nobility, the stage was set for the successful invasion from the south.

Musa ibn Nusair, conqueror of Morocco, Tangier and Ceuta, the last vestiges of Roman authority in North Africa, organized the invasion of the Peninsula ostensibly in response to the request of Yulyan (Julian), a Christian Berber who governed Ceuta. The governor sought to avenge the dishonoring of his daughter by the Visigoth king, Roderick. The accounts tell of a lovely Florinda, who had been sent to Toledo for schooling, a custom widely shared by the Muslim and Christian illuminati of the time. She was reportedly abducted and deflowered by the young Visigoth King Roderick. Julian's request for revenge, coupled with his descriptions of a land rich in natural resources, gold and silver, and divided by intrigue and religious disaffection among the oppressed Jewish and Hispano Romano populations, interested Musa.

Concerned by the arrival of displaced exiles from the thwarted Jewish rebellion and the growing population of the tribes of newly converted Berber warriors who had gathered outside of Ceuta, Musa acquired permission from the Caliph of Damascus and appointed Tarif ibn Malluk to lead an expeditionary force of three hundred soldiers. After his successful preliminary expedition along the coast, Tarik ibn Ziyad, governor of Tangier, crossed with an invasion force of seven thousand men. Setting his encampment on a site known as Jubal-Tarik, contemporary Gibraltar, Tarik attacked the Christian settlements along the coast. King Roderick, apprised of the invasion, abandoned his campaign against rebels in Pamplona and headed south, gathering troops and allies along the way. Tarik fortified his positions along the coast and awaited the arrival of the Christian forces. On the 19th of July in the year 711, Tarik's Berbers met and defeated Roderick, whose forces were plagued by internal dissent and abandoned by their serfs and slaves. King Roderick's fate was unclear. He either drowned in the Barbate River, site of the battle, or fled this military disaster, abandoning his kingdom to the Muslim forces. The deserted Visigoth capital of Toledo, formerly overseen by the archbishop of Spain, Sindared, was occupied in the same year.

Musa crossed the Straights of Gibraltar in June of 712 with an army of eighteen thousand troops, joined the forces of Tarik, and liberated the Jews and Christians who had aligned themselves with the invading Muslims. With the fall of the city of Merida after a six-month siege, Muslim hegemony of the southern Spain was assured. Christian Visigoth Spain crumbled.

A new Muslim religious and cultural reality had been established which a century later would foster an environment conducive to the transformation of the legendary figure of Santiago. The nascent Christian unity of the Reconquest would soon mirror Muslim religious militancy by claiming the intercession of a legendary figure at the battle of Clavijo in 844. St. James, the martyred apostle, who had an ever-widely disseminated historical narrative, would be transformed. James, the Greater, Spain's Santiago of Compostela, would become *Santiago, el Matamoros* - the Moor Slayer.

Pilgrim's Staff Changed to a Sword
Reflection: Our semblance is not unchanging.

You will lead me by the right road though I may know nothing about it.
Therefore will I trust you always though I may seem to be lost
And in the shadow of death.
Thomas Merton (1915-1968), A Prayer

James, the Greater, the crusading champion of the faith, reappeared in the legends and historical narrative of Spain's early Middle Ages. James' legendary participation in the battle of Clavijo added a new dimension to the persona of the patron saint of Spain. Letting fall his pilgrim's cloak, he stepped out as the holy warrior; Santiago, the Moor Slayer, *el Matamoros*. The historic military encounter occurred in 844 or 845 between Ramiro I of Asturias and Abd al-Rahmán III, emir of Córdoba.

Legend maintains that a peace accord between the two kingdoms required tribute from the Christian kingdom in the account of 100 virgins. Ramiro I refused to comply with the terms of the truce and a battle ensued at Clavijo. The Muslim army punished the Christian forces the first day. The Christian king announced on the morning of the second day of battle that he dreamed that Santiago counseled him on military tactics, assured him of a Christian victory, and promised to accompany him in combat. Legend maintains that a knight bathed in light, riding a white mount and carrying a white banner with a red cross, led the charge. The ensuing Christian victory was attributed to Santiago de Compostela.

St. James reappeared in 939 at the side of the troops of Ramiro II at Simancas, battling against the invading Moors who were led by Abderrraham III, Caliph of Córdoba. During this military encounter, St. James rode through the clouds carrying a miter, crosier, and a sword. St. Millán accompanied him in battle. Gonzalo Bercero described the saints as "the white horsemen that ride white steeds, the knights of God."

St. James' resplendent figure also appeared in battles against enemies from the north. Invading Norsemen had pillaged the northwest Atlantic coast of the Peninsula since the 9th century. The citizens of Compostela in 968, chaffing under the Norsemen's two year occupation of their city, rallied around St. James who again rode against Christian Spain's enemies. The battle cry, *Santiago! Cierra España, St. James! Close ranks. Forward, Spain* would be heard on the battlefields of Piedrahita in 959, Coimbra in 1064, and Ciudad Rodrigo in 1173 when a  similar visage of this resplendent figure on a white horse was reportedly seen during hostilities. Santiago's apparition would be chronicled over 38 times during the Reconquest and the Age of Discovery.

Cortés and his conquistadors sought his intervention during the Battle of Otumba, and considered it received when the retreating Spanish survivors rallied and turned back the army of Cuauhtémoc. St. James appeared among the ranks of the beleaguered Spaniards, and reportedly inflicted horrible losses on the Aztec troops. Similarly, Pizarro and his troops sought divine intercession against Atahualpa in Cajamarca, Perú and vanquished an Incan enemy force of forty thousand warriors. (Starkie, 44)

Almanzor at the Foot of the Tomb
Reflection: Defeat accompanies victory.

I went on for several hundred yards ... till I came right under it at last;
And with the hesitation that befits all great actions I entered,
Putting the right foot first lest I should bring further misfortune upon the capital
of all our fortunes. And so the journey ended.
Hilaire Belloc, *The Path to Rome,* 1958, p. 231

St. James did not always prevail against the invader. The razing of St. James' cathedral by the forces of Almanzor, last of the great generals of the Umayyad Caliphate in Córdoba was a case in point. Mohammed Abi Amir, an ambitious young man descended from a Yemenite family, would ascend in influence through cunning and intrigue in the court of Caliph Hakam II, son of Hasdai. The lover of the Caliph's favorite wife, Abi Amir became master of the mint of Córdoba, manager of the estate of the crown prince, and royal chamberlain. Though descended from generations of judges, not warriors, Abi Amir became known to his Christian and North African Arab enemies as al-Manzur al Allah, *"the Victorious by the grace of God"*, a skillful military tactician, a severe disciplinarian, and ruthless conqueror. (Bendiner, *The Rise and Fall of Paradise*, 226-231) His annual raids of the northern Christian territories brought slaves, tribute, prisoners, and, most assuredly, enhanced Almanzor's well-cultivated image of conqueror.

During one of his last military campaigns, Almanzor stood at the foot of the tomb of Santiago. Departing from the city of Córdoba on July 3, 997, he headed north to Galicia with his calvary. His infantry and supplies sailed down the Guadalquivir to the Gulf of Cadiz, out into the Atlantic and proceeded north along the Portuguese coast. (232) His cavalry and infantry met at Oporto and marched to the Miñon River. Muslim troops cleared roadways through the forests and mountains of Cantabrian Cordillera, and within the following month, his troops overlooked the city of Compostela and the spires of its cathedral.

On the 10th of August in 997, Almanzor entered an abandoned Compostela. His troops systematically razed the city and dismantled the cathedral stone by stone. Legends vary concerning the events of the entrance into the Christian city. Some accounts maintain that the invader respected the cathedral and its surrounding precincts, including the apostle's crypt. Other histories tell of the destruction of the great cathedral with the exception of the saint's tomb. Moorish chroniclers recount that the demolishing of the cathedral and its surrounding precincts was so devastating that not a trace of the cathedral remained. Recent archaeological investigations indicate that the entire church was fired and gutted at the end of the 10th century.

Almanzor's scorn for the shrine's precincts was well documented by Muslim historians. Riding into the sanctuary, the military commander watered his horse from the cathedral's baptismal font. He forced Christian slaves to carry the sanctuary's bells on their backs to the Grand Mosque in Córdoba. The cathedral would be rebuilt by 1128 during the time of Bishop Diego Peláez and King Alfonso VI. The very same bells would be returned on the backs of Muslim prisoners after Ferdinand III, The Saint, conquered the city of Córdoba in 1236.

All of the accounts include the episode of Almanzor's encounter with a solitary monk who remained behind during the initial occupation of the city, piously kneeling in front of the saint's tomb. Popular legend holds that upon entering the cathedral, Almanzor confronted an old monk who was praying before the apostle's tomb. Starkie recreates the encounter:

"Who are you and what are you doing here?" demanded al Mansur.
"I am a familiar of St. James and I am saying my prayers," said the old man.
"Pray on as you wish. No man shall molest you," responded al Mansur.
(Starkie, 28)

Impressed by the cleric's faith and perhaps fearful of the magic of the stone of the Apostle's tomb, Almanzor forbade the killing of the holy man and set a guard around the precincts of the apostle's tomb, sparing the relic's stone enclosure. (Bendiner, 234) Some local histories claim that the saint's remains had already been spirited out of Compostela by Bishop Pedro Mezonzo shortly before Almanzor's arrival.

Although many accounts portrayed Almanzor as respectful, yet unfazed by the mystical persona of James, one episode common to the St. James lore depicted a conqueror aware of the apostle's magical powers. After dismounting to survey the demolition of the cathedral, Almanzor gave instructions to have his horse watered at the cathedral's baptismal font. The conqueror's horse reportedly entered the temple's precincts, drank from the sacred font, and immediately exploded, causing panic and flight among the invaders.

Further conquests during this successful Muslim campaign would provide Christian prisoners who would carry Compostela's cathedral bells and metal gates to the Great Mosque in Córdoba. The bells would be suspended upside down as trophies and reminders of Allah's greatness, and Almanzor's military prowess. The gates were melted down and made into lamps for the mosque. The great *al-Manzur al Allah* would return to Córdoba and his palace, *Madīnat al-Zahrā*, *"beautiful town of Zahra"*, and reign for another five years. He succumbed to an undiagnosed illness in the field during a military campaign against Castile in 1002 and was buried in Medinaceli. (234-235)

Santiago bolstered Spanish military morale and forged a link between Spanish Catholicism and future military endeavors. The Christian equivalent of a warrior holy man had been realized. His divine intercession legitimized Christian claims on the newly conquered territories south of the Cantabrian Mountains, and spiritually validated Spanish monastic militarism. Santiago offered the Christians a divine standard-bearer, conqueror and redeemer, a worker of miracles, and chastiser of infidels. The melding of nationalism and religion and militarism with piety set the groundwork for future relations between the Catholic Church and the emerging Spanish state. The Reconquest moved forward under the cross and image of the apostle. Accounts cite how he encharged Ramiro I with the protection of Christendom's expanding realm:

"N.S. Jhesu Cristo partía todos los otros apóstoles, mis hermanos, et a mí, todas las otras provincias de la tierra, et a mí solo dió a

España que la guardasse et la amparasse de manos de los enemigos
de la fe "

Santiago de Compostela had become *Santiago El Matamoros*, the
Moor Slayer, and the undisputed patron saint of an emerging, unified
Christian Spain.

Chapter 5
THE *WAYS* THOUGH THE AGES

Ancient Mercantile Routes
Reflection: Answers found in the past
weigh more than future's promise.

When, then, I not only saw with the sense of sight those Sacred Places, but I saw
the tokens of places like them, plain in yourselves as well, I was filled with joy so
great that the description of its blessing is beyond the power of utterance.
Gregory of Nyssa, 'Letter XVII', cited in H. Wace & P. Schaff, eds., *A Select*
Library of Nicene and Post-Nicene Fathers of the Christian Church, Vol. V:
Gregory of Nyssa, 1893, p. 542

A trans-peninsula commercial route that passed through Galicia and connected the Mediterranean and the Atlantic existed for several millennia. The northwest corner of Hispania served as a source of valuable metals during the first and second millennium before Christ. The Iberian Peninsula, considered a source of raw materials by many pre-Roman civilizations, figured prominently in mercantile routes which funneled copper, tin, silver, and gold from the British Isles, Gaul, and the mines in Galicia to foreign ports in the eastern Mediterranean. Ancient commercial land routes, running west to east, paralleled the medieval *Way* of St. James.

Galicia figured prominently in an inter-continental mercantile route that crossed the north of the Iberian Peninsula from the Atlantic to the Mediterranean at the beginning of the Bronze Age. Galician tin, much sought after by Bronze Age metallurgists, flowed along the northern land route, facilitating mercantile as well as cultural intercourse between the British Isles and the eastern Mediterranean cultures. Galicia, the center of this thriving metallurgy industry and conduit for these exchanges, was the source of the *mater prima* as well as the crossroads of this ancient interregional commerce route. (Luis G. de Valdeavellano, *Historia de España: De los orígenes a la baja Edad Media*, 110-111)

Predating the Roman presence and the Celtic migrations, stand the megalithic Bronze Age cultures of the Peninsula, dating from 1900 to 1250 BC. A crescent-shaped area, unique in culture and technology, ran from the Montelavar Horizon Culture in Central Atlantic Portugal, up the northwest coast through Galicia, and turned east through the Cantabrian and Basque regions and southeast into Navarra and Aragón. Numerous examples of sophisticated metallurgy and megalithic architecture characterize the littoral cultural zone of the Atlantic Bay of Biscay. The concentration of dolmens and menhirs along the coast of Portugal and the Basque-Navarra region, where megalithic architecture reached its zenith, signal the presence of a significant Bronze Age culture. Abundant remains of metallurgy in the form of swords, jewelry, pendants, spears, and bracelets particularly in Galicia, speak of a cultural zone densely populated and connected along a commercial route, whose directionality ran from the east to the west coasts of the Iberian Peninsula. (Montenegro, 14 -15)

The north and northwest of the Peninsula had a history of intensive occupation by many cultures and tribes. Pre-Roman urban settlements were connected by their own commercial and sacro-religious routes that extended from the western coast to the east to the Spanish Mediterranean and over the Pyrenees to the south eastern coast of France. As these Celt Iberian, Celtic, Austre, Cantabri and Gallaecian settlements fell to Roman armies, they became stopover points on the Roman highway's trajectory from Mediterranean ports to the Atlantic coast.

The Roman highway system, which crisscrossed the Peninsula connected *Barcino,* Barcelona, in the Levant with points west, passing the provincial capitals of *Caesaraugusta,* Zaragoza, and *Lucus Augusta,* Lugo, and *Brigantium*, former Gallaecian capital and terminating in *Caronium,* A Coruña, on the Atlantic coast. Although not identical to the St. James' pathway, many of the former, smaller Roman cities and settlements, which figured in the Imperial highway system, appear along the *Way of St. James.* Unfortunately, the Roman encampment and settlement, which would eventually become Compostela, fail to appear on Imperial highway maps. The existence of a Bronze Age commercial route with west-east directionality predated the presence of Christianity by dozens of centuries and paralleled or overlaid the pilgrimage route of St. James.

Medieval Pilgrimage Routes
Reflection: We neither carry the same weight nor walk the same path as others.

Give me my scallop shell of quiet, my staff of faith to walk upon,
My scrip of joy, immortal diet, my bottle of salvation,
My gown of glory, hope's true gage, and thus I'll take my pilgrimage.
Sir Walter Raleigh, 'The Passionate Man's Pilgrimage', *The Faber Book of Religious Verse* (1972), p.76

Pilgrims of the Middle Ages selected various points of entry into Spain and followed eight major routes of different lengths and difficulty; all characterized by different degrees of self-sacrifice and danger. The pilgrimage route to Santiago de Compostela would become the most frequented pilgrimage system in Europe. The Peninsula-crossing medieval ways and routes originated in different parts of Spain and Portugal and formed an elaborate system of intersecting tributary routes, which directed pilgrims from Italy and Provence, Germany, France, England, and Flanders to the tomb of the apostle.

The shrine of St. James rivaled those of the Holy City of Jerusalem and Rome. His pilgrims grew to outnumber the *palmers* who traveled to the Holy Land and the *romers* who journeyed to Rome. The popularity of St. James' relics surpassed those of St. Joseph of Arimethea, located at Glastonbury, St. Thomas of Canterbury in

England, and St. Martin of Tours in France. Pilgrims journeying along the route saw above them the *Milky Way*, a celestial band of stars, which during certain seasons appeared to follow the east-west directionality of the pilgrimage route. Popular belief held that souls of deceased pilgrims journeyed along the celestial pathway of the *Via Lactea*. The occasional shooting star represented the spirit of an errant pilgrim and was accompanied by the saying, *"Dios te guie y la Magdalena"*. (Munro, *Glory Road*, 184-188)

Leanor Munro points out in her work *On Glory Roads: A Pilgrim's Book about Pilgrimage* that the imagery of the Way found common expression irrespective of the pilgrim's country of origin. The characteristic dark caps, criss-crossed with lines of white shells, wide capes with peaked hoods, large wooden rosary beads, a walking stick, and the scallop shell pendant characterized the medieval pilgrims' garb. Statuary along the route had common motifs as well. Depictions of pilgrims, sporting outfits frequently identified with alchemists and astrologers of the early Middle Ages, and statues of the familiar figure of St. James wearing his cloak and broad tri-corned hat with an oak staff in hand achieved wide distribution along the pilgrimage route. Even the facades of buildings along the Way had the scallop shell motif.

The earliest routes, the French Way and the North Way, entered from France and crossed the Pyrenees at three major points: Hondarribia, Roncesvalles and Santa Cristina (Port of Somport). Traffic along these highways waxed and waned according to the success of the Reconquest effort and reports of Saracen raids. The *Camino del Norte*, the North Way, fed through the small port of Hondarribia and led pilgrims safely away from the Muslim raiding parties which forayed along the more frequented and direct *Camino Francés*, the French Way. However, the northern-most coastal route was not trouble-free. Pirates and Vikings who raided coastal settlements made the journey perilous during the late 9th and 10th centuries.

Pilgrims, who chose the *Camino Francés*, entered Spain through the pass at Roncesvalles or Port of Somport and Santa

Cristina, the most eastern points of entry. These two routes merged at Queen's Bridge, *Puente de la Reina,* and headed west through the small town of Estella. This northern roadway passed through the coastal cities of Donostia-San Sebastian, Bilbao, and Santander and turned southwest to Oviedo, the first capital of Visigoth Spain.[21] The route bifurcated into the *Road of Fontsagrada* that headed southwest through Lugo and Palas de Rei, passing through Arzú terminating in the shrine. The other secondary route of the North Way continued along the coast and skirted any southern route until reaching Barrieros. A second bifurcation occurred which directed the more hesitant traveler northwest to A Coruña and south along the English Road, *Camino Inglés,* or moved traffic south at Barrieros, passing numerous towns, finally turning west again at Arzé, where it would link up with the Fontsagrada route.

Four major overland French routes, originating in Paris, Vezelay, Le Puy, and Arles, funneled pilgrims over the Pyrenees and onto the northern-most extension of the Camino Francés. The *Via Tolosana* which was known as the *"Roman Road of Hercules"* departed from the cities of Genoa and Turin and followed the coast through San Remo and Nice, Italy crossing Provence, passing the Rhone Delta through the cities of Aix, Marseilles, and Arles. A route, which crossed Catalonia, the northeastern region of Spain, included stops at the shrine of the Black Virgin at Montserrat and at the Church of Our Lady of the Pillar in Zaragoza.

The *Via Podiensis* carried German pilgrims through Burgundy, Avvergne, and crossed the Languedoc and Gascony regions. Pilgrims originating in Flanders would join fellow travelers from Paris, Orleans, Tours, Poitiers and Bordeaux, and head south along the *Via Turonesis.* French pilgrims from western and central France followed the *Via Lemosina.* (Munro, 186)

Although the French Way was the most frequented and direct of all the routes, it was subject to more danger and frequent interruptions due to its proximity to the ever-shifting militarized zone between *Al Andaluz* and Christian Spain. Today's contemporary route follows this

---

[21] The Camara Santa of Oviedo's cathedral was considered by many to maintain the most precious collection of relics found anywhere in Spain. The cathedral's fame was immortalized by the Asturian proverb; "To visit Santiago and not Oviedo was to pay homage to the servant and not the master."

main road established in the Middle Ages that followed the legendary pass at Roncesvalles and led down through northern Spain via the cities of Pamplona, Logroño, Burgos, and León, linking up with the *Portuguese Road* at Palas de Rei. The French Way was protected by the Templars, the famed warrior monks, and maintained by the French Benedictine order of Cluny. As the expansion of Christian controlled territory pushed south towards Toledo, this became the preferred and most transited of all the routes.

The southernmost course, the Silver Way, know as *Via de la Plata*, began in the formerly Muslim-controlled *Al Andaluz*. The Christian-controlled *Andalucía* opened to Christian pilgrims after the fall of Sevilla in 1248 by Ferdinand III, the Saint. The Silver Route extended south through Zamora and Salamanca and passed through the Extremadurian cities of Mérida and Cáceres, terminating in the recently liberated cities of Cordoba and Sevilla. King Alfonso X, who returned the bells of the shrine's Cathedral taken by Muslims in 997, led the first pilgrimage from Sevilla.

The Portuguese Way, *Camino Portugués*, moved up from the south and entered Spain at Tui and passed north through Pontevedra. Travelers from southern Portugal, the Canary Islands or Northern Africa entered through the Maritime Route of Arousa, *Ruta de Mar de Arusa*. These pilgrims took the Galician *rías* inland for over twenty miles, disembarking at any number of ports, and moved northeast to the shrine through Padrón.

Others spent the initial stages of their journey aboard chartered ships from England. Maritime routes from England and southwestern France facilitated a quick and relatively safe passage to the shrine. The ships deposited the faithful in the cities of A Coruña; Ponte-deume, and points southwest of Neda. The English Way, *Camino Inglés*, led inland and south over a relatively short and direct route to Compostela. These maritime routes frequently carried English and Scandinavian pilgrims whose pilgrimage circuit began with Compostela, included Jerusalem, and ended in Rome.

The final maritime route, which embarked from England, landed at Muxia and zigzagged along the Galician coastline south to Finisterre/Fisterra. The roadway followed two divergent inland routes, which linked up at Muros on the coast and headed to the shrine through Noia, and north to Negreira. Perhaps this route served as a post-pilgrimage exit from Santiago of Compostela as well. Templar mercantile interests, whose growing fleet gave safe, albeit expensive passage to the influential and wealthy, monopolized the pilgrimage sea routes.

The *Camino Fisterra-Muxía* which connected many ancient, pre-Christian mythological sites might have been a terminus for some pilgrims who considered the major shrine not to be the Cathedral of Compostela, but rather the bluffs of Finisterre, the legendary *End of the World.* Alchemists, esotericists, and perhaps, Muslims of the Middle Ages walked the *Way of St. James.* These non-Christians considered Compostela to be one of the many sacred sites found along the *Way of the Stars,* concluding their pilgrimage at Cape Finisterre, site of the mystical union of water and sky. (Alexander Roob. *The Hermetic Museum: Alchemy and Mysticism*, 700-701)

Ancient Ones along the Way
Reflection: The Sacred Way remains after we have gone.

Walking is the proper speed and the proper posture that can prepare man to meditate ... But that which is holy must be approached slowly.
Kosuke Koyama, *Pilgrim or Tourist* (1974), pp. 1-3

Pilgrims have traversed the contemporary Way of St. James for millennia. After the official recognition of the discovery of the apostle's tomb and remains, the city of Compostela joined Rome and Jerusalem as one of the three most sacred sites of pilgrimage in all of Christendom. Millions visited the crypt of James beginning in the mid-9th century. Northern European pilgrims called Spain of the late 9th and 10th centuries *Jakobsland*, the land of Santiago. But Christians were not the first to walk the paths and byways of today's pilgrimage route.

The religious symbols, chants and prayers, sacred garments and cosmological visions varied over dozens of centuries, but the pathway provided the common thread which fused thousands of years of spiritual activity. The regions through which this spiritual route passes have long been considered lands of myth and esoterica with their own distinct magico-religious histories. Long before the Romanization of this region, and epochs before the arrival of the Iberians, a well-traveled route cut across the top of the Iberian Peninsula, connecting the Mediterranean and Atlantic coasts. Initially, this pathway represented the migratory route of animals, often pursued by hunters from the numerous prehistoric populations that inhabited this region. Paleolithic huntsmen followed the animals' movement along the Peninsula and associated this route with a plentiful food source. Neolithic peoples of the Cantabrian Mountains traveled along the path to Pyrenean grottos in southeastern France. Their return trip west followed the sun as it sunk into the waters of the Atlantic. Bronze Age peoples of the Mediterranean Levante developed a commercial route that linked ancient Atlantic cultures with those of the Mediterranean. Caravans would follow these routes, connecting peoples and cultures of the Atlantic and Mediterranean.

Numerous populations entered Spain through passes in the Pyrenees. Indo European peoples who penetrated from the north before 1,000 BC moved southwest along the pathway. Celtic migrations in the 7th century BC followed these northern tracts and reached the Atlantic coastal region of Galicia. The Suevis and Austres, Visigoth tribes entered from southern France in 409 AD followed the direction of the *Way* and resettled the northwestern tip of the Peninsula. A firmament of pre-Christian peoples traveled the route passing the same streams and grottos, under the shadows of the same mountains that today's pilgrims admire.

The route has always been multiple and diverse, much like its pilgrims; followers of ancient cults and disparate religions, faithful to a myriad of deities, seekers of truth and enlightenment, aspirants of self-renewal, and ritualized spiritual death and rebirth. Ancient pilgrimage tracts criss-crossed the Iberian Peninsula from Spain's temperate northeast, the wind swept and mercurial central *meseta* region, and the southwestern flank, crossing the desert-like regions of Extremadura. Many routes have ended at the site of the current shrine, yet others passed it, heading to the original terminus of the *Way of Stars*, Finisterre, a bluff overlooking the Atlantic, the end of the known world.

Shared Myths and Visions at the Ends of the World
Reflection: Your interior voice will know the way.

*Pre-Christian religion seems to have had an intense feeling for this rhythm of
the seasons ... this idea clings, even when its meaning is forgotten; dour Scotts
still climb Arthur's Seat in Edinburgh to bathe in the dew on May morning ...*
Daphne Pochin Mould, *Irish Pilgrimage* (1955), pp. 56-57

The tradition of pilgrimage along an ancient spiritual pathway is
not unique to Spain. France has its equivalent *camino de estrellas*,
pathway of the stars, which terminates on bluffs that overlook the
Atlantic. *Findes Terres* in Brittany, and Galicia's *Finisterre* figured
in ancient pilgrimages to what was known in Celtic mythology as
the termini of the known world and the point of departure to the
Land of the Dead. Today, these sites have churches for contemporary
religious and secular activity, but these ancient ends of the world
also share similar accounts of proto-historic religious rites, Bronze
Age monolithic architecture and comparable narrative structures in
their local legends. Ancient people of divergent ethnic and cultural
backgrounds occupied these venues and developed parallel visions of
the cosmos. The promontories of these *Ways* gave ancient man vistas
of the other world where the sun's warmth and light disappeared into
the depths of the sea; the source of fecundity and darkness, gravitas
and jubilance, death and rebirth. These routes to the Otherworld
ultimately led to the innermost corners of the human psyche and
spirituality.

Common to *Findes Terres* and *Finisterre* are topographical
features associated with cataclysmic, diluvial events. *Monte Aro*
in Galicia and Brittany's *Montes Arée* provide settings for the
legendary repopulation of the planet by a Noah-like cultural hero
that disembarked on or near these mountains' summits, disseminated
language, stone working, culture, and architecture to the people that
he encountered. Legends recount the journey that the new arrival
undertook, leading his followers to higher ground. Though tradition
and legend fail to identify the route they might have taken, prehistoric
rock drawings may speak to this legendary history. Petroglyphs of
spiral-like designs appear on rock outcroppings at these sites, and

hint at the possibility of an original spiritual pathway that was walked from the coast inland by these regions' legendary inhabitants.

Megalithic architectural sites with menhirs and dolmens are scattered along these routes of the stars. Tapered menhirs, individual monumental stones vertically positioned, were sites of magico-religious activity for Bronze Age peoples. Dolmens, ancient burial chambers made of boulders arranged in a tripod configuration with a lintel stone slab as a roof, appear along these spiritual pathways. These megalithic structures common to the British Isles, Brittany, the Iberian Peninsula, the Balearic Islands of Mallorca and Menorca, and Malta were the architectural vernacular of a Bronze Age culture whose genesis could be found in the Mediterranean.

Pre-Christian fertility rituals were conducted at *Findes Terres* and *Finisterre*. At both sites, the megalithic architecture of the area provided settings for this ritual activity. At the Galician *Finisterre*, the promontories of *Artabros* and *Monte Nerium* were sites of fertility rites. The Celts and the Gauls believed that stones of these termini were imbued with mystical, life-generating powers. According to the Roman historians, Plinio and Estrabón, childless couples would face the sea and copulate on altar-like ledges or on the roof lintenls of dolmens while Celtic priests intoned prayers to the cosmos. In Brittany, legend maintained that the early Gauls encouraged their barren women to rub their loins and stomachs on the vertical shafts of stone menhirs.

Both locales are associated with cities that either sunk into the waters of the Atlantic or disappeared. In Brittany, the mythic *Yu* was swallowed by the sea and the legendary *Duyo* or *Dugium* was entombed by the sands of the Galician coastline. Historical figures caused these cataclysmic events when their apostasy offended divine powers. In Brittany, the destruction of the ancient menhirs by the recently baptized daughter of a Gaelic king provoked the wrath of the cosmos. Likewise, a Galician king was engulfed by a sandstorm when he pursued disciples of Saint James.

Marian iconography found in these sites dates from the early Christian epoch. A substratum of pre-Christian motifs in goddess statuary points to a Venus-Aphrodite cult at these sites. Marian cults dedicated to black or dark skinned Madonnas figure in accounts that involve the Spanish apostle, James and Saint Cornelius of Brittany. The black virgin venerated in Soulac, Brittany, known as *Notre-Dame de Findes Terres*, is the undisputed icon of the region. *Nuestra Señora de Finisterre* of Galicia parallels the black Virgin of Soulac.

The Galician counterpart was introduced in the 1100's, venerated in the church of Santa Maria, lost in the 16th century, and replaced in 1646 by a statue carved by Francisco Anta. The church of *Santa Maria de Iria Flavia* claims to have housed and displayed the 12th century black Madonna of Galicia. These Marian cults dedicated to black virgins might reflect a more distant past whose view of the cosmos has syncretically fused with current Christianity. The black virgin cult found in certain areas of Europe could be an extension of a widespread pre-Christian, earth mother cult characteristic of Neolithic and Bronze Age peoples. Medieval alchemy may have contributed to the historical magico-religious overlay of the Marian cults of these two areas. The purposeful rendering of the virgin in black or dark stone or wood is reminiscent of the black liquid produced by the alchemist Philosopher's Stone.

Both sites have proto-Christian accountings of visits by sacred personages. Persecution, flight, miraculous escape, and transformation characterize these stories. Saint Cornelius, pursued by pagan soldiers, fled in an ox-drawn wagon to a bluff overlooking the Atlantic. Failing to escape his pursuers, Cornelius hid inside the ear of one of the oxen, and with divine intervention, transformed his pursuers into stone. The rocky outcroppings and menhirs of Carnacare are known as *les sourdadets saint Cornley;* the soldiers of Saint Cornelius. A church marks the spot of this miraculous transformation of flesh into stone, and hosts an annual pilgrimage during the second week of September. Accompanied by livestock, the locals make pilgrimage from their town and around the church, following the path of the setting sun. Popular belief maintains that the soldiers reanimate on Christmas, descend to drink from nearby fountains, and at dawn, are frozen again in stone.

A similar history that chronicled the travails of St. James involves a hermitage located at an ancient Roman burial spot, Padrón-Iria Flavia; terminus point of one of the many Galician rías. James, fleeing his pagan persecutors, mounted an ox and headed to a cliff facing the Atlantic. The saint dismounted and began to scale the mount. Unable to escape the soldiers, he struck the mountainside with his *bacilli*, walking staff, and asked for divine intervention. Miraculously, the mountain opened and James found refuge in a newly formed cavity. His attackers fled upon seeing the miracle, but saint's wrath transformed them into boulders. Local legend contends that the night of the feast of Saint John, the 24th of June, the soldiers reappear and dance around the bonfires of Saint John, before returning to stone in the early morning.

Martin de Tour *beatus patronus* of Galicia
Reflection: May your deeds stand taller than your words.

We have touched the soil and rocks where the seed falls.
We have seen the lilies of the field and heard the birds of the air.
We have been warmed by the sun that warmed him and
Cooled by the breezes that touched his face.
Stepen Doyle OFM, cited in Margaret Pawley, *Prayers for Pilgrims*
(1991), p. 132

A widespread saint cult dedicated to a 4th century cleric existed several hundred years before the discovery of St. James' tomb and the development of the St. James legendary history. The cult dedicated to St. Martin of Tours (372-397) born in the province of Pannonia, contemporary Hungary, figured prominently in the history of the early Church in northwestern Spain and northern Portugal. Devotion to Martin of Tours was widespread in the Pyrenean region of France and Spain, and the See of Tours became a popular site for pilgrimage from the 4th to the 6th centuries. Martin de Tours was known to be a man of great virtue that performed miracles and extraordinary feats of faith.

Hydatius mentions that Martin of Tours was associated with Ambrose of Milan, contemporaries of Priscillian. Martin and Ambrose were opponents of the Priscillian sect. During Priscillian's heresy trial Martin de Tours actively debated the heretical doctrines of the Bishop of Avila. At the conclusion of the dissident theologian's trial, Martin requested that Emperor Maximus stay Priscillian's execution. The emperor carried out the death sentence only after the death of Martin of Tours. After Martin's death, devotees reported miracles and began pilgrimages to Tours. Gregory of Tours, Bishop of Tours promoted the cult of St. Martin. The earliest mention of a shrine dedicated to Martin of Tours dates from the middle of the 6th century AD.

The rise of this saint cult is attributed to Galicia's close contacts with the developed world of that time and the efforts of Martin Braga, missionary to the Sueves of northwestern Hispania. During the first and second centuries AD the development of Roman Galicia was due to its contact with the Mediterranean basin and the region of Lusitania in Portugal. Galicia's strong commercial and cultural connection to Lusitania and the Mediterranean allowed for the entry of religious and philosophical movements prevalent in both of these regions. The entry of the Martin de Tours cult into Spain was a direct result of these contacts during the late Roman period, the years of Germanic invasions and France's Merovingian period during the 6th century.[22]

The widespread devotion to Martin of Tours stems from the efforts of the missionary Martin of Braga (520-579), the Bishop of Iria Flavia who bore witness to the popularity of the cult in his *Chronicon*, which covers events from 378-469. Martin of Braga arrived in Galicia around 556. Braga, who evangelized the Sueves, promoted the St. Martin de Tour cult among these peoples.

The success of the early Church was due in large part to the efforts of Martin of Braga. He founded monasteries, converted the Arian Sueves to Catholicism, and wrote a number of pastoral and theological works. The popularity of the St. Martin cult can be attributed to Braga's efforts that promoted the cult of the saint and popularized stories of St. Martin's curative powers. Venantius Fortunatus, Bishop of Poitiers, 530-600, recounts the 30 years of evangelism of Martin of Braga in Galicia and his devotion to and efforts to promote the Martin of Tours cult in Galicia.

According to regional legendary history, the relics of Martin of Tours cured the Arian King Chararic's son of leprosy. When the grateful king erected a church in honor of Martin of Tours and rejected Arianism in favor of Catholicism, the disease disappeared from all of Galicia. Martin of Tours was declared the blessed patron,

---

[22] Alberto Ferreiro, *The Pilgrimage to Compostela in the Middle Ages: A Book of Essays*

beatus patronus, of Galicia by Gregory of Tours. The Suevi kings adopted Martin of Tours as their patron and protector at Braga, their capital, and built the first shrine in honor of the saint.

Similar to the St. James cult, the legendary history of St. Martin of Tours includes divine military intervention. According to local history, Leovigild, Visigoth Arian king and archenemy of the Sueves, attacked a Catholic monastery where only a single cleric remained. The lone monk continued to pray, unaffected by the invader's arrival. The pious cleric was set upon by the Visigoths, but suffered no harm. His attackers died instantly, struck down by the powers of St. Martin of Tours.

The Displacement of Martin de Tours
Reflection: The unexpected changes us.

Life be in my speech,
Sense in what I say,
The bloom of cherries on my lips,
Till I come back again.
Oliver Davies & Fiona Bowie, *Celtic Christian Spirituality,* (1995), p. 128

The disappearance of the saint cult dedicated to Martin of Tours coincided with the demise of the Suevi kingdom, which was destroyed in 585 by Visigoth Arians. The conquest of the Sueves, followers of Martin de Tours, signaled the ascendency of Arianism in the northwest of Hispania and the decline of the saint's popularity. Catholicism returned to Galicia in 589 when Recared, son of the conqueror, Leovigild, rejected Arianism and proclaimed all of Hispania to be Catholic at the Third Council of Toledo. Although three hundred years would pass before the discovery of St. James' tomb, Christianity's return to Galicia would provide fertile ground for the eventual continuation of a saint cult phenomenon.

The success of the Muslim invasion provided a catalyst for the Santiago cult. With the rise of small and ambitious kingdoms in the north of Spain which challenged the hegemony of the Muslim expansion, a divine military icon with a universal appeal proved useful. These emerging kingdoms in the north required a formidable divine opponent whose military protection and intervention they could invoke against the Muslim invaders. Although the legendary history of Martin of Tours included the protection of the monk, he was perceived as a provincial religious figure. The Church authorities needed a religious icon whose affiliation and appeal was less provincial and more national.

With the announcement of the discovery of the tomb in Compostela, the Carolingian Empire began inquiries into the Santiago history, hoping to find its own patron and protector for the royal court. The reported appearance of St. James at Clavijo further interested the Court. The archbishop of Asturias-Galicia quickly adopted Santiago to prevent the Carolingians from claiming him as their patron. The final displacement of St. Martin of Tours was complete.

Chapter 6
HIS CHALLENGE TO ROME

Compostela's Archbishop Rises with St. James
Reflection: Let generosity, not vanity, fill the void.

And the pious man will be counted as insane, and the impious honored as wise
... the one afraid will be considered strong ... and the good man punished like a
criminal.
Nag Hammadi version of the Hermetic dialogue Asklepios, The Gnostics,
Churton, pg. 63

Compostela and Rome were distant spiritual spheres of influence, which vied for control of Christendom in the 10th and 11th centuries. The moral vacuity and flawed spiritual leadership of Rome disenchanted many regional Church leaders of the early Middle Ages. On the other hand, the papacy considered the Spanish cult of St. James to exceed simple veneration and represent the continuation of pre-Christian religious beliefs. Rome felt threatened by Compostela's growing international popularity and its resistence to the implementation of a universal Church doctrine. Notwithstanding the syncretic and integrative nature of many of the doctrinal components of the emerging Catholic Church, James' cult embodied a direct challenge to the authority of the Roman Catholic Church.

The archbishops of Santiago de Compostela, spurred on by the intrigues, the ineffectiveness and corruption of the papacy in the 10th and early 11th centuries, became more assertive. The faltering leadership of the Church, attributed to papal debauchery and petty tyrannies, bolstered the claims of Compostela's prelates to spiritual supremacy. After all, Compostela had the relics of an internationally venerated apostle and enjoyed increasing international exposure. (Castro, 110)

The official acknowledgment of the presence of the apostle's relics, the international notoriety of the pilgrimage route, and the subsequent increase of prestige of the shrine at Compostela, began to rival the traditional religious centers of Rome and Jerusalem. The shrine's popularity gave credence to local sentiment that the legitimate center of Christendom was Galicia's Compostela. By the tenth century the bishops of Compostela, emboldened by the shrine's popularity and the growing financial rewards of the ever-popular pilgrimage, claimed titles of eminence, fitting only the papacy of Rome. Ordoño III claimed the title *totius orbis antistiti* in 954 and effectively began a rivalry with Rome's authority. Bishop San Rosendo followed suit and claimed the title of Bishop of the Apostolic See, publicly declaring primacy in the Church of Spain in 974. Pope Leon IX threatened the Bishop Cresconio with excommunication during the Sinid of Reims in 1049 citing his inappropriate claims to authority,

"porque contra el derecho divino vindicaba para sí la cúspide del nombre apostólico." (Valdeavellano, 694)

The fragility of Rome encouraged the Archbishop Diego Gelmírez (1100-1140) to claim papal authority over the Spanish Church and consider Compostela the actual center of a rival papal empire. The Archbishop appropriated the role of a papal authority, receiving pilgrims with pontifical airs and honors. Assuming the powers of the pontificate, he named cardinals, continued to use the local Mozarabic rite at mass, and received pilgrims as *"Apostolico more"*, thus assuming papal right. (Castro, 109-111)

The separatist sentiments in Compostela, popular during the later part of the 10th century, compounded papal suspicion of Spanish orthodoxy. The Papacy in the early 11th century categorized Spain as a dissident outpost of antiquated and provincial rites with a long-standing history of heretical beliefs. The Peninsula's history of heretics and esoteric and unorthodox interpretations of the scriptures confirmed Rome's suspicions.

Heresy and the Early Spanish Church
Reflection: Find common ground in difference.

God of the nomad and the pilgrim, may we find our security in you and not in our possessions. May our homes be open to guests and our hearts to one another so that all our traveling is lighter and together we reach the goal.
Mary Batchelor, ed. *The Lion Prayer Collection* (1992), p.139

Priscillian, native of Avila, Spain represented the first serious challenge to the Pauline teachings of the early Church. Bishop of Avila who was decapitated in 385 by the Emperor Maximo, Priscillian openly espoused the apocraphal *Acts of St.Thomas* and the twinship of Jesus. He was accused of "Gnosticism and questionable sexual liberties." (Alberto Ferriero, *The Cult of Saints and Divine Patronage in Gallaecia before Santiago, Book of Essays*, Dunn and Davidson, 4) Reportedly born in Iria Flavia in the 4th century, this Spanish cleric reportedly practiced a heretical form of Christianity, astrology, and a form of magic once characteristic of the Celts of this region.

Trade routes controlled by Syrian shipping interests introduced Nazarene thought to the Mediterranean ports of Spain and southern France. These teachings which formed the corpus of Priscillian's beliefs required strict adherence to Judaic law, insisted on a mortal and natural birth of Jesus, and maintained that the Messiahship of Jesus was terrestrial and the fulfillment of a biblical kingly bloodline. Priscillian began his teaching in the south of Spain and traveled extensively through Iberia and Gaul. His most fervent followers were in *Gallaecia*.

Priscillian actively sought out hidden Thomasine texts, which espoused the mortality of Jesus and maintained the existence of fraternal links between Jesus and several of his apostles. This ascetic professed belief in numerology and other Cabalistic teachings. He celebrated the Sabbath on Saturday, denounced the Trinity, and questioned the divinity of Jesus. The popularity of Priscillian's teachings challenged the Pauline-dominated doctrine of the early Church. Ambrose of Milan, Pope Damasus and Martin of Tours challenged Priscillian's heretical beliefs. Martin of Tours later became the focus of a Galician-based saint cult, which preceded St. James by three hundred years. (Ferreiro, *Essays*, 5)

An oral tradition paralleling the St. James legendary history claims that the body of Priscillian, retrieved from his execution site at Trier, was transported to Galicia, the land where his heresy flourished. Claiming him to be their regional martyr, the local Galician population enshrined his body and recognized his tomb as a site of pilgrimage. In his work, written in 1976, *Priscillian of Avila,* Henry Chadwick of Oxford University, put forth the thesis that the route used to return this executed heretic home was the genesis for the pilgrimage tradition in Galicia, and that his remains were located under the floors of the Cathedral of Compostela. (Chadwick, 233) The most recent excavations conducted in Santiago revealed several 4th and 5th century seplucra, which faced east towards Jerusalem. The followers of Priscillian worshiped facing east during their group devotions. On a final and even more curious note, the authors of *Messianic Legacy*, Biaget, Leigh and Lincoln, citing Juan G. Atienza, a contemporary historian and specialist on Spanish esoterica, state that the *French Way* is actually the route which the disciples of Priscillian used as they returned to Galicia with the body of their spiritual mentor. (Biaget, Leigh and Lincoln, *Messianic Legacy*, 115)

The Manichaean heresy proliferated in Christian countries in the 4th and 5th centuries, threatening Roman orthodoxy. Manichaean schools in Spain espoused Gnostic dualism, the doctrine of reincarnation, a metaphorical interpretation of Jesus' divinity, and the belief that Jesus survived a staged crucifixion. (Biaget, Leigh and Lincoln, *Holy Blood, Holy Grail*, 385) These enclaves followed the teachings of Mani, who in 240 AD became known as a prophet, healer and exorcist. He claimed enlightenment from the same heavenly source as Zarathustra, Buddha and Jesus. Known as the Savior and progeny of a virgin birth, Mani evangelized throughout the Middle East. The dichotomy of light and darkness, evil and benevolence formed his cosmological vision. The Gnostic dualism of Manichaeism espoused reincarnation, and considered Jesus to be a mortal who survived his crucifixion. Mani suffered flaying, decapitation, and dismemberment in 276 AD. Public display of his remains failed to prevent the propagation of his teachings that spread throughout the Middle East and the Mediterranean basin.

Arianism of the Visigoths displaced Roman doctrine in Spain in the early 400s. Although monotheistic, Arianism insisted on the mortality of Jesus and denied the existence of the Trinity. Arius proposed a monotheistic concept of a single Supreme Being who did not undergo incarnation or suffer a physical death. Jesus was recognized as a "*Messenger of God*", and, like many of the mortal prophets, evangelized in the name of the Supreme Being. Founded on Judaic teachings, which precluded the divinity of Jesus, Arianism was widely accepted by the Germanic tribes of the Goths, the Suevi, the Alans, the Lombards and ultimately, the Visigoth monarchs of Spain. Although Spain returned to Trinitarian Catholicism, following the martyrdom of Hermenegild in 589 AD and the conversion of his brother Recared I, the first Catholic King of Spain, the history of persecution of Spanish Christians at the hands of the Visigoth Arians formed part of the Spanish heretical tradition recalled by the Roman papacy.

Cluniacs in Ascendancy
Reflection: Compliance fosters singularity,
but life resides in plurality.

It is deliberate sundering and surrendering of one's habitual conditions of comfort, routine, safety and convenience ... the pilgrim breaks with his material servitude ... and sets out on a quest which is inward as much as outward, and which is, in varying degrees, into the unknown.
Social Anthology of Pilgrimage, ed. Makhan Jha (1991), p. 302

The papal instability and its moral shortcomings during the 10th century gave way to a papacy capable of presenting an image of strength and doctrinal purity. Rome in the 11th century resolved to unify Christendom under its auspices and universalize Roman doctrine. Seeking to bolster and expand papal hegemony in the Peninsula, the Roman Church sought to eliminate autonomous, liturgical rites and establish a universally practiced Christian doctrine and expression. The papacies of Alexander II and Gregory VII and the monastic orders of Cluny aided by the Cistercians pressed for this doctrinal singularity. The Visigoth monarchy of the Peninsula initially resisted.

The Benedictine monks of the Order of Cluny founded in 909 AD represented a monastic tradition supportive of papal concerns, and directed their efforts to universalize Roman rites among the kingdoms of Europe. The Visigoth *Mozarabic* or *Toledian Rites* practiced by Iberian Christians stood in contradiction of papal initiatives to universalize Roman doctrine. Religious tolerance characterized Moorish rule in *Al Andaluz* where Christians enjoyed a level of religious tolerance unknown in the Christian north. Catholics who lived under Muslim rule were called *Mostarabuna* or *Arabizants* and their liturgical rites were known as Mixt-Arabic or Mozarabic. These Mozarabic rites, inherited from the Visigoth Catholicism with Arian and Byzantine elements and rewritten by St. Isidore and Leander of Seville, SS. Ildefonso and St. Eugenius of Toledo, conflicted with the doctrinal hegemony sought after by the Order of Cluny and Pope Gregory VII.

Mozarabic hymns, prayers and variations of the mass peculiar to the Christianity of the Peninsula formed a rite of longer duration than that of the traditional Roman mass. The rite addressed the Virgin Mary directly in prayer, used ashes during the liturgical celebrations of the Church, and required numerous responsories between the celebrant and the congregants. The Benedictines considered this rite to be aberrant, antiquated, heretical, and contrary to the internationalist initiative of the Holy See.

The internationalization of the pilgrimage route to Compostela, the preponderance of French pilgrims in the 11th and 12th centuries and the receptiveness of the King of Navarra (Aragón), Sancho the Great (1028-1035) and his sons García of Navarra and Fernando of Castille to the Order of Cluny in disseminating the Roman rites in the Peninsula began the transformation of Spain's spiritual landscape. The acquiescence of local prelates solidified the Order's enclaves in La Rioja and Castile, and foreshadowed the spiritual and doctrinal hegemony that the Order would soon enjoy. The papacy of Alexander II achieved the first replacement of the Toledian rite in Spain. Encouraged by King Sancho's embracing of the Order's ideals, Cardinal Hugo Cándido of Aragón, legate of Pope Alexander II, was the first to introduce the rite in the monastery of San Juan de la Peña in 1071. (Pidal, La España del Cid, *Historia de España*, 463)

After the death of Alexander II, Hildebrand, a former Cluny monk, ascended to the Holy See taking the name Pope Gregory VII. He aggressively pursued the adoption of the universal Roman rite in Christian Spain. Concurrently, the papacy claimed its right to tribute and submission from Spain through a legendary gift of the Peninsula by Emperor Constantine to the early Church. King Alfonso VI repudiated these papal claims forestalling foreign control over Spanish national sovereignty, but compromised on the doctrinal issue promising that the Roman rite would be adopted before his death.

Notwithstanding Alfonso's acquiescence, the papal initiative to universalize the Roman rite continued. Pope Gregory pressed the Spanish regent, requesting on March 19, 1073 that he respect his promise to abandon the regional rite of mass in favor of the universal

Roman rite. The king, reacting to a current of popular resistance to this measure, delayed its introduction.

Saint Hugo de Cluny, admired by King Alfonso, pressed the Spanish monarch to align himself with the papacy. Alfonso annually paid over two thousand gold pieces to the Order, considered Hugo and the Order *mei fratres carissimi*. In the interim the death of the monarch's wife, Queen Inés, preoccupied the crown for over a year. A Cluny abbot of the monastery of San Valerín arranged Alfonso's second marriage to Constanza, the granddaughter of Robert II, king of France and daughter of Robert the Old and Duke of Burgundy. Following the arrival of Constanza, Bernard of Sauvetat in Perigord, a Cluny monk, former knight and confidant of the new French-born queen enjoyed considerable influence and position in Spain, being named abbot of the monastery in Sahuagán.

The Order, whose influence was solidified by royal marriage, pursued the liturgical change. Compelled by his affection and respect for Cluny and his promise to adopt the Roman rite, King Alfonso VI acceded to the pope's request and in the spring of 1080 the Council of Burgos abolished the practice of the Mozarabic rite and declared the Roman rite to be Spain's. Popular resistance to French doctrinal supremacy failed in Castille and national adoption soon followed. Shortly thereafter, Roman control was complete when the traditional Toledian characters previously taught and used in Spanish monasteries were replaced by French handwriting taught by the Cluniacs.

The universal adoption of the Roman Rites, the initiatives of the Spanish crown to Europeanize Spain, and the significant monastic presence of the Order of Cluny in northern Spain diminished the unique nature of Spanish Christianity, and fomented a national acceptance of Rome's authority. The Cluniacs, custodians of the pilgrimage route, reaffirmed Europe's access to the shrine in Compostela within a new Romanized context. Cluny monks propagated the legendary acts of the apostle, aided in the construction of hospitals and sanctuaries for pilgrims, and sought to provide a safer environment for pilgrimage.

In contrast to the demise of Compostela's rivalry to papal authority and the unique character of Spanish Catholicism, the spiritual and historical legitimacy of St. James and his shrine were enhanced. The Spanish royalty, needful of pilgrims' foreign currency, encouraged the development of local industries that encouraged the growth of pilgrimage. Local Church scholars recanted the Spanish Church's denunciations of the presence of the historical St. James; national Church authorities fully endorsed new liturgical rites as the Spanish clergy embraced the representatives and teachings of the Order of Cluny. The French monastic Order, custodians of the new Spanish spirituality, maintained the Way of St. James, linking Spain to universally endorsed religious practices as well as foreign political interests.

Terrain Loses to Destination
Reflection: Know the path, before seeking the destination.

"The Christian emphasis on persons symbolized by objects was superimposed on a much older tradition of pilgrimage to places that were holy in their own right, often because some natural feature such as height, water source or grotto was considered to have sacred power. Churchmen decried the ancient notion that natural site features were sacred."
Hugh Nibley, Jerusalem, (1973), p. 291.

The abandonment of the Mozarabic rite and the imposition of teachings of the Order of Cluny helped transform the popular understanding of ritual pilgrimage along St. James' *Way*. As the early Church struggled to achieve doctrinal universality over regional heresies, the popular acceptance of the sacrality of the Way's terrain concerned Church authorities. The reverence for the pilgrimage's sacred terrain and its pre-Christian associations became anathema to the emerging dogma of the Catholic Church. The ascendency of the Cluniacs assured the decline of the route's ancient, cosmological associations. Church leaders tied their emerging doctrines to pre-existing sacred routes, and modified oral histories with doctrinally acceptable ones, and supplanted cosmological personages with more contemporary and doctrinally current and acceptable ones. The dual, integrative character of ritual pilgrimage that correlated sacrality with natural surroundings was changed. The symmetry of ritual pilgrimage, whose components of movement and permanence, the passage through venues and final destination, terrain and its sacrality, which were integral to the ancient pilgrimage rite, began to disappear.

The animist nature of the *Way* ceased to be self-validating. Terrain could no longer be sacred, rather a viaduct which was simply directional. Destination became prominent. Edifice supplanted nature. Cathedrals and chapels replaced grottos, streams, and rock outcroppings. The Order of Cluny undertook an expansive building program financed by St. James' lucrative pilgrimage route. Chapels, hospitals, and churches appeared along the route with an emphasis on doctrinal singularity and practicality. The universality of the religious icons, as well as incorporating local pagan motifs and iconography into religious architecture, helped achieve the Order's mission. The assimilation and renaming of ancient, pre-Christian deities and their sites homogenized the sacred venue and its pre-Christian significance.

The directional character of the route was emphasized and the innate spiritual rewards of traversing the path sublimated. The sacrality of the course was superseded by the Church's need for arrival; a destination that housed holy relics was paramount. The duality and balance between sacred line walking, mystic terrain, and destination were modified. Singularity, not duality, characterized the ritual act. Hegemony and universality triumphed over plurality and multiplicity of belief and iconography. Destination and travel along roadways supplanted movement over sacred terrain.

St. James' Popularity Declines
Reflection: Recognition and fame may have the life of a flame.

"Quien muchas romerías andas, tarde o nunca se sanctifica."
He that on pilgrimage goeth becometh holy late or never.
Popular 18th century Spanish saying

Christian hegemony was established in the Peninsula on January 2, 1492 with the taking of Granada and the flight of Boabdil, the city's last Masrid ruler. Granada's fall signaled the end of the Reconquest. Spain entered the Age of Discovery and the figure of St. James' and his pilgrimage began to recede from the public stage. His decline in importance and prestige paralleled the drop in the numbers of foreign pilgrims who visited his tomb. International, commercial activity became less dependent "on the guide of religion" and less tied to the regional cottage industries spawned by foreign travelers along the pilgrimage route. (Starkie, 46)

The humanist philosophers, most particularly Erasmus, John of Colet, and Rabelais, questioned the spiritual validity of relics and the Church's interpretation of the miraculous. Many 16th century Spanish philosophers decried the vacuousness and basest nature of pilgrimage and gave voice to the growing disbelief and disillusionment with saint cults and their relics. Seen through the eyes of a Europe entering the Age of Protestantism, paying homage to saints' relics was not an act of piety, but rather institutionalized idolatry. Critics maintained that pilgrimage led to habits of actual endless wandering and "vagrancy not at all tending to edification" leading scholars of the day to proclaim, *"Qui varia invisiti peregrinus limina temple Innocuus vita, cum vagus est. Minime!"* (*Notes and queries*, Volume 12, July-December, 1855)

A growing number of Spanish clerics, historians and distinguished writers of the 1500s called into doubt the authenticity of the St. James's relics and presented cases against his presence in the Peninsula. The historian and cleric, Juan de Mariana, questioned the accepted Church history of St. James in Spain. The Archbishop of Toledo, García de Loaysa, in a document of the Lateran Council, denied James' historical presence in Spain. Cervantes lampooned Spain's saint cults. The establishment of the University of Compostela in 1526 by Archbishop Alfonso III of Fonseca failed to stem the decline in popularity of pilgrimage to the saint's cathedral and tomb. The disappearance of the saint's relics shortly before the incursion of Drake and their continued sequestering, until the 19th century, contributed to the disaffection among the intellectual establishment.

Rival religious factions in the Spanish Church challenged St. James' devotional monopoly. The Virgin of Guadalupe and St. Joseph grew in popularity. The Discalced Carmelites championed the cause of Saint Theresa of Avila, proposing that she be named Co-Patron of Spain. The mysticism of St. Theresa of Jesus and St. John of the Cross focused on the values of physical labor, solitude, and humble asceticism and led to a profound spiritual enlightenment free of public displays of piety. Pilgrimage was anathema to the teachings of Spain's mystics. Philip III and the Council of Castile accepted this proposal, ordaining her as Patron of Spain in 1620. A national firestorm of public debate resulted and Pope Urban VII intervened, declaring St. James the Greater, the one and only Patron Saint of Spain. St. James had survived the controversy and entered the 1700s unscathed. Pilgrimage to Santiago's tomb waxed and waned during the course of the 18th century. Urban progressive thought in Spanish society considered pilgrimage a curious regional custom and a religious anachronism.

The turbulence of the 19th century drastically reduced pilgrimage to the Cathedral of Compostela. International conflicts and the introduction of anticlerical international philosophies threatened the pilgrimage tradition. The invasion of Spain by France in 1802 and the subsequent outbreak of the War of Independence interrupted the flow of pilgrims to Compostela. The presence of Spanish, English, and French armies in the north and the clandestine movement of Spanish guerrillas discouraged the movement of pilgrims to Compostela.

Devotion to Santiago declined with the rise of regional autonomy movements in Catalonia and Galicia. Contrary to the efforts of Rosalía Castro and the brief intellectual resurgence known as the *Rexurdimento* during the later half of the 19th century, the conservative and isolated character of the city further contributed to its backwater, provincial image and its saint's pilgrimage, a medieval oddity.

The reappearance of the saint's relics on the 29th of January in 1879, and the subsequent reconstruction of the crypt briefly directed the nation's focus to Compostela. Initial archaeological investigations conducted during this time revealed the presence of a Roman tomb typical of the first and second centuries. The original burial site had a large anteroom and a smaller chamber for the sepulcher. The reconstructed tomb was positioned immediately above the ancient Roman funerary structure. Physicians from the Faculty of Medicine at Compostela University reconstructed and catalogued the remains of three bodies, which were re-entombed in July of 1884.[23] The archaeological discovery of the relics failed to recapture the prestige and fame of the site. The nation's political clouds overshadowed what was considered a quaint, ecclesiastic activity in isolated Galicia.

---

[23] The silver urn, designed by Losada and cast by Rey y Martínez, was divided into compartments that separated and contained the remains of three bodies. The crypt's design attempted to approximate the original Roman tomb.

The introduction of the anticlerical, international philosophies, such as anarchism and communism, affected the religiosity of the urban and rural populations. Urban workers employed in the industries of Spain's major cities were drawn to the rising syndicalist movement. The rural poor became progressively more politicized as the anarchist philosophy of Michael Bakunin began to take root. The cult of St. James and pilgrimage to his resting place fell into disuse and became a curious anachronism in the late 19th century.

Chapter 7
INTERPRETATIONS OF THE SANTIAGO CULT

Stars, Terrain and the Generation of Myth
Reflection: Night's light nourishes.

I believe it is a constellation; you become simply one of the thousands and
thousands of stars within it.... A star may be sharp and full of pain, but it may
also be a guide, a useful companion on a dark night.
Jini Fiennes, *On Pilgrimage: A Time to Seek,* 1991, p. xi

Ancient man's field of vision was multiple; horizontal and vertical, terrestrial and celestial, focused on earth and sky. Early man sought a deeper understanding of the natural world that nourished and astonished him. The landscape which he inhabited, populated with predators and game animals, comprised of water sources, rock shelters and natural resources, and subjected to the unpredictable natural phenomena of nature. His encounters with this ever-changing environment compelled him to render meaningful nature's forms and iterate understandings of variable natural phenomena.

A significant corpus of celestial knowledge figured in the compendium of information of early man. The initial impulse to gather, collate, and interpret data about the heavens was tied to food gathering and survival. Evan Hadingham in his *Early Man and the Cosmos* noted that the progression of the seasons and the migrations of game would provide the initial impulse to invest time and effort to catalogue and form associations with star fields, earthly topography, and food-gathering activity. Acquiring information and its subsequent interpretation would be initially tied to the need to survive. (Hadingham, *Early Man and the Cosmos*, 50) Hadingham observes, *"His focus would have incorporated the changing night skies in his emerging cosmological visions."*(48) The genesis of the ritual act of pilgrimage may have been linked to a single astronomical principle and later tied to terrestrial markers, which reflected or represented the night-sky phenomenon.

Early man imposed on seemingly capricious external phenomena a structure that gave reason and order to the inexplicable. This construct known as the Ur-Myth or the Myth of Cosmos viewed the world as a Cosmogonic Egg, a spherical envelopment of physical and non-physical environments in which man operated. A terrestrial plane that divides a planetary-solar-stellar field from a subterranean abyss intersects in the Cosmogonic Egg. The sky was paternal, solar, and light-filled. The earth was maternal, dark and lunar. The separation of the two after coitus was the eternal phallus, a cosmic axis that spanned the divide. The celestial and terrestrial fields joined through a World Tree or Axis Mundi, which provided a point of confluence, ascendency, and descent.

An astral connection to the St. James history becomes more apparent as one examines the Essene sect which influenced James and Jesus. Sacred astrology and astronomy focused on the Polestar, a guiding astral point of reference whose presence and predictability was coordinated with their festal and ritual calendars. The polestar, which marked the actual North Pole of the earth, was conceived as the errant creator, whose pilgrimage through the heavens was chartered by ancient sages worldwide. This was the star sought after by Abram. The astrologers of Quarum, the Essene community in Galilee, would have similarly focused on this celestial phenomenon. The magi followed closely an astral event that led them to the birthplace of Jesus. Not coincidentally, stars figured prominently in the discovery of St. James' tomb.

The origins of the St. James legendary history are based on an understanding of the role of this astral phenomenon, its mythic nature, and the role of the divine intermediary structures, which tied the celestial progenitor with terrestrial domains. These ties, known as *hinges*, connected the divine plane with the earth via mythical, divine figures. These earthly guardians were imbued with a sacred humanity which allowed them to move among humanity. Cosmological narrative structures were generated which identified them with the stars and natural phenomena such as thunder and lightening. These terrestrial guardians linked man with the heavens. These *hinges* folded the heavens to earth, and materialized in sacred terrain, man-made monuments and, most importantly, in mythological and historical personages. These figures were frequently paired, one affiliated with the heavens, the other with the terrestrial domain. The Gemini twins, Pollux and Castor, Romulus and Remus, children of the She-wolf, and the brothers *Boanegres*, James the Greater and John the Evangelist, were sons of Intemperate Weather, Children of Lightning and Thunder, the *Boanerges*.

The origins of sky myths are found in the rising of the sun in the house of Gemini, the twin stars, Castor and Pollux. Hindus call them *asvins*; the ancient Greeks called them *Dioscuris*. These sacred, human pairs, progeny of the gods or other divine humans, figured in a sacred geometry centered on a triad. A divine male triad, composed of a central figure and two sacred earth representatives, created a triangular structure that supported the universe on terrestrial points on earth. The Dioscuri pairs manifest themselves in the legendary history of Santiago de Compostela in the persons of James and his brother, John.

These mythic structures and their affiliated celestial phenomenon are not invariable. Their visibility from earth and their apparent position of ascendency in the night skies are subject to change. Earth's alignment with stars that have served as the mythic Polestar has changed. Although the actual points of celestial reference vary due to this movement, the practice of Polestar observation and affiliation with the divine remains constant. The cyclical narrative of the Polestar and its divine twins, Sun-twins and their humanly divine hinge pairs with their extra-human affiliations and powers ascend, decline, disappear, and reemerge.

The Dioscuri
Reflection: The center brings order and structure to chaos.

"...a pilgrimage is a journey to a sacred place which lies beyond the mundane realm of the pilgrim's daily experience ... considered to be the cosmic center ... the world beyond the world ... an axis mundi of his faith ... that pilgrimage can be thought ... the private, mystical journey made public, a journey of the spirit which is physically enacted."
John Eade & Michael Sallnow, eds. *Contesting the Sacred,* (1991), p.78

James and his brother John are perhaps the last manifestation of the celestial doubles known as *Dioscuri*. The fraternal celestial pairs who intervened in military encounters appear frequently in Roman and Greek mythologies and early Church histories. The themes of personages with brilliant luminescence, accompanied by an equestrian element that directly participates in the military endeavors of their followers are common to these classical traditions. Myth, legend, and ancient religious belief merge in the tradition of the Divine Pair or *Dios-kuroi*. The fraternally linked pair of apostles, James and John, and the predominance of pairs of saints in Spain's early Christian history mirror the mythological pair of brothers, Castor and Pollux and this *Dioscuri* tradition.

The intervention of Castor and Pollux forms part of Roman military lore. The Romans were devotees of these heavenly twins who were believed to aid their followers on the battlefield. Known to the Greeks as Castor and Polydeuces, these divine twins were born of Leda, an Aetolian princess. Zeus, considered to have sired the twins, appeared in the guise of a swan and seduced Leda. The twins hatched from an egg laid by Leda. Pollux shares his immortality with Castor who fell fatally wounded in one of their adventures, and revives his dying brother. Zeus requires that the twins travel between the heavens and the Earth as humankind's protectors. The Romans named them the "sons of thunder", *Boanegres,* the progeny of Jupiter.

James and John of Zebedee were known as the brothers *Boanegres*. This Semitic expression comprised of bn 'son' in Hebrew, while *bnaym* means 'sons' or *bney*; the term *rges* corresponds to the term *ra'am'* or thunder', *rayasca* in Arabic meaning to thunder. The brothers *Boanegres* continuing the *Dioscuri* tradition of the celestial pair signified "sons of Thundering Jupiter" or *Bana-ba Tilo,* "sons of the heavens". The Father Thunder, the divine paternal head of the brothers, continues the ancient structure of nature divinities. The father-head of ancient mythology formed the sacred triad of *Celestial Father* affiliated with the sun and light and his *terrestrial sons* tied to star fields. In the case of the brothers James and John, their father Zebedee, was considered to be a powerful member of his community and an astrologer whose purported control over the elements and extra-normal abilities may have earned him the title *Father of Thunder.* The *Boanegres* title given to the brothers may have been a reference to the man who sired them.

If the *Thunder Father* was patterned after the classic dyads of the Mesopotamian *Ba'al/Yahweh* or the classical *Zeus/Jupiter* he would have been associated with an astronomical phenomenon that might have been the Polestar. Castor and Pollux, sons of Zeus, found their celestial home in Gemini. St. James considered the *astro brillante de España,* "the brillant star of Spain" associated with Sirius which for a 3,000 year period rose along the 35th parallel on July 25th, the Feast Day of St. James aligned with his pilgrimage route. (Munro, *On Glory Roads,* 48)

The personal attributes ascribed to the brothers *Boanegres* evoke the storm-thunder personages of Ba'als and Yahweh and the storm clouds of the Hellenic Zeus and Rome's Jupiter. These intemperate divine forces of nature hurled thunderbolts appeared incarnate among both men and women and intervened in Man's terrestrial affairs. The biblical account of the sons of Zebedee requesting permission of Jesus to call down fire from heaven on unrelenting pagans ties them to the Dioscuri tradition. Eleanor Munro observes in *On Glory Roads: A Pilgrim's Book about Pilgrimage* that the Stone Age tools found during the Middle Ages were considered to be materialized thunderbolts and were called *Zebedee stones.*

Castor and Pollux, a divine pair that intervened in military encounters, mounted white horses and subdued the enemies of Rome. These ancient mythological sons of Jupiter appeared to the Roman dictator Postumio in 499 BC at the battle of Lake Regilo along the

Via Salaria assuring him a resounding military victory. Castor and Pollux, luminescent and mounted on white horses, joined battle against Rome's enemies and assured victory for Postumio and his legions.

G.G. King pointed out in her work of 1920 *The Way of St. James* the parallels between Ibero-Roman mythical iconography and portrayals of St. James in the early Middle Ages. Castor appears on Iberian coins with a lance in hand and thunder bolts on the opposite side of the coin. He was also strongly identified with an equestrian-divinity theme. The Hippodrome of Olympia reportedly had at its entrance an altar dedicated to these equestrian divinities. Inscriptions dedicated to Pollux have been found in Baetis as cited in the work of Toutain, *In Les cultes paines dans l'Empire Romain.* The very title given to the sons of Zebedee by Jesus, the characteristics of thunder, resplendent figures and light associated with the appearance of St. James on the battlefield whose thematic quality is reminiscent of the appearances of Castor and Pollux, the early Spanish Christian tradition which paired Saints James and Millan, and the singular figure of St. James on white mounts exemplifies the classic tradition of *Dioscuri*.

Alfonso, El Sabio in his *Crónica General* portrays St. James of Compostela as acting and appearing as a *Dioscuri*. His narration depicts the saint as seated on a white horse with a shinning sword and white garments. Ramiro I attributes the divine intervention in vanquishing the Moors at Clavijo:

"veerm'edes cras andar y en la lid, en un cavallo blanco, con una seña blanca et grand espada reluzient en la mano."

A variant form of a similar apparition occurs at the battle of Simancas in 939 AD According to the 13th century study by Gonzalo de Berceo *The Life of Saint Millan*, Saints James, the Greater and Millan aid the numerically outnumbered Christian forces to defeat the Saracens. The account states:

"... vieron dues personas fermosas e lucientes, mucho eran mas blancas que las nieves recientes. Viníen en dos cavallos plus blancos que crista l...avíen caras angélicas, celestial figura,

descendían por el aer a una grant pressura, catando a los moros
con torva catadura, espadas sobre mano, un signo de pavura."

The concept of the divine pairs appears throughout Roman Catholic Martyrology. Numerous pairs of saints figure in many of the accounts of the early Spanish Church and popular regional folklore; Saints Cosmas and Damian, twin brothers from Arabia who studied medicine in Syria; apostles Andrew and Peter, Saints Paul and Barnabas, Philip and Bartholomew and the sons of Alphaeus, Matthew and James. A.H. Krappe in his 1932 article *Spanish Twin Cults* highlights the preponderance of pairs of saints from the Peninsula. Alfonso III mentions in his *Crónica General* the small sanctuary dedicated to the twin saints Facundo and Primitivo located near the banks of the Ceya River that runs along a section of the Way of St. James. The presence of the divine double appears in an examination of Spanish martyrs; Justa and Rufina, Justo and Pastor, Emerterio and Celedonio. These saintly pairs martyred during the earlier years of the Spanish Church and the popular history of the divine double echo the *Dioscuri* structure, so common in the mythology of the pre-Christian world.

Few of these divine pairs or the individuals who comprised them ever reached the revered position attained by St. James the Greater. Due to a highly regionalized belief in a divine twinship between Jesus and one of the apostles also named James, the early Spanish Church ascribed a shared parentage between Jesus and Spain's *Dioscuri*, Santiago de Compostela.

St. James as a Reflection of the Divinity
Reflection: Find yourself in others.

So here I am, a pilgrim through life, restless indeed, looking, searching all the
time for that which will make me truly and fully myself.
Basil Hume, *To Be A Pilgrim* (1984), p. 39

The belief that Jesus had a fraternal double who shared in his divinity figured in some early Christian traditions and subsequent heretical movements. The existence of two separate individuals named James in the Gospels, scriptural references to Apostolic genealogies linking one of them to Jesus and the Thomasine apocrypha writings encouraged the belief in the divine double and a blood fraternity between Jesus and some of his apostles. Popular traditions and beliefs of the Spanish Church seem to have consolidated the two separate Jameses into one apostolic entity in the person of St. James of Compostela.

References to a fraternal link between Jesus and other apostles appear frequently in scripture. James the Lesser is named the brother of Jesus. Scriptural references associated this apostle with Jesus and also named his mother as Mary:

"Is not this the son of the carpenter, the son of Mary, the brother of James, Joseph, Jude and Simon?" (Mark 6:3; cr. Matt.13: 55)

James the Lesser worked with Matthew collecting taxes. They were identified as *sons of Alphaeus.* Marriage may have provided a link between the families of Joseph and Alphaeus and in this sense James and Jesus may have been first cousins. Scholars of the Semitic languages indicate that *brother* may have been used in the sense of a *relative*.

James the Lesser, who referred to himself as "James, the servant of God and of our Lord Jesus Christ" headed the Jerusalem Church in the early years after the crucifixion of Jesus. The deferential treatment which Peter and the other apostles accorded James the Lesser coupled with his influential position in the early Christian community of Jerusalem indicates his close ties to the founder of the nascent Christian movement.

Falvius Josephus, a Jewish historian of the first century AD, recorded the trial and stoning of James the Lesser in 62 AD and clearly indicated a widely recognized genealogical link to Jesus:

"Assembled the Sanhedrin of judges and brought before them James, the brother of Jesus who was called the Christ, and some of his companions; and when he had laid accusations against them as breakers of the law, he delivered them to be stoned." (Antiquities of the Jews, Book 20, Chapter 9, 1)

The scriptural references to fraternity with Jesus, which specifically mentioned an apostle named James, were interpreted by the early prelates of the Spanish Church as a direct reference to the James of Compostela. The distinguishing epitet of *ho mikros*, "the runt" or "the small one" was overlooked. Commonly interpreted in this fashion, scripture seemed to proclaim Jesus' codivinity to be the Sant Yago, St. James the Greater, the historical Jacob bar Zebedee.

The cult of the divine brother entailed an acceptance of common parentage and, thus, strong physical resemblance. The belief that Jesus had a twin brother developed in Syria and Palestine. The Fourth Gospel refers to St. Thomas as *Didymus*, the twin. References to Thomas, meaning "twin" in Syrian, as *aptum artificem*, ascribed to his apparent striking physical similarity to Jesus, appear in early Church writings and lore. He was known as *Thomas apostolus Christi, Didymus nominatus, et juxta Latinam linguam Christi geminus, ac similis Salvatoris.* (Rendel Harris, *The Twelve Apsotles*, Cambridge, 1927)

Eusebius of Caesarea indicates that St. Thomas was also called Judas Thomas. The Syrians knew him as *Judas the Twin*. The apocryphal Acts of Thomas use both names, Thomas and Judas, clearly referring to one person, *"Whilst Judas was reasoning thus, our Lord appeared to him in a vision of the night, and said to him ... Fear not Thomas!"*

The Acts of Thomas appear to maintain the twinship of Judas Thomas or Jude the Twin with Jesus. Scripture indicate several encounters in which the evangelized confuse Jesus with Judas Thomas, perhaps due to their uncanny physical similarity. Such confusion appears in the first Act of Thomas when Jesus responds to the inquiries of a young bridegroom saying, "I am not Judas, who is also Thomas, I am his brother".

The Mozarabic rite of the Hispanic Church incorporated New Testament apocrypha and underscored the concept of divine brotherhood of Jesus and Judas Thomas. Priscillian, Bishop of Avila, who openly declared the apostle Judas Thomas to be Didymus Domini, the twin brother of Jesus, popularized these early Christian and proto-Christian writings (Americo Castro, *España en su Historia*, 127)

Scriptures that appeared to iterate the existence of a divine twin, be he Thomas or one of the Jameses, fostered a belief that Jesus did indeed have siblings one of whom might have visited and even been buried in the Iberian Peninsula. Many prelates of the early Spanish Church held the belief that James, the Greater shared parentage and codivinity with Jesus. Although the Church fathers and later authorities interpreted this fraternal link as spiritual and symbolic, the popular Spanish interpretation appeared to give credence to a biological parentage. Common reading of scripture bolstered St. James' codivinity with Jesus. Matthew was frequently quoted as saying in 13: 55, "Is this not the son of the Carpenter. And are his brothers not called James and Joseph?"

St. James' codivinity with Jesus formed part of the early Spanish Church's St. James tradition. The followers of St. James in the early years of the cult maintained that James was not only *"the son of thunder"*, but also the brother of Jesus. In the early 10th century, the relics in Compostela were considered those of the son of Joseph, the Carpenter. Pilgrimage was done to the shrine of *Sancti Jacobi, germani Domini* in the first centuries of the cult. Even the Arab historian, Ibn Hazm in his Critical History of Religious Ideas, cites the belief that James, the Greater, was the brother of Jesus. Ibn Idari in his *History of Africa and Spain* written in the 13th century commented:

"Some Christians say that Santiago was the son of Joseph, the Carpenter ... The devoted come to his temple from Nubia, the country of the Coptics."

During the course of the national debates surrounding the naming of Saint Theresa of Avila the Co-Patron of Spain, Bishop Gelmírez answered the Carmelites by making a direct reference to these early beliefs. Gelmírez referred to James' blood fraternity to Jesus by saying, *"Cristo quiso que el patronato fuese de su primo solamente"* (Christ Himself insisted that Spain's Patron should be His cousin alone.) (Starkie, *The Road to Santiago*, 57) These popular beliefs either enjoyed acceptance in the hierarchy of the Church of Spain, or were recognized as being so widely held by the general public that Gelmírez felt comfortable defending challenges against St. James by publicly acknowledging popular lore, incorporating them into his defense of St. James.

A parallel tradition associated St. James of Compostela with James the Lesser, first bishop of Jerusalem who is often referred to as the actual blood brother of Jesus. Regional and local accounts assigned the same parentage and histories to both. Americo Castro points out in *España en su Historia* that this composite James, codivinity, brother of Christ and evangelizer of Hispania eventually became the St. James of Compostela in Spanish popular legend. This amalgam of legend, arcane versions of the gospels, and a regional, idiosyncratic interpretation of the scriptures reinforced the belief of St. James' codivinity with Jesus. The original feast day of St. James the Greater was the 25th of March; the same day Christ's passion was commemorated. This further underscored the deeply held belief in codivinity. Later, the feast date would be reassigned to the 25th of July in order to defuse this heretical belief. Perhaps this date reveals an even more ancient tradition of *Dioscuri* alignment with star fields. James' Feast Day coincided with Sirius rising above the pilgrimage route on July 25th.

Chapter 8
EARLY MAN AND SACRED PATHWAYS

The Sacred Reveals Itself
Reflection: The Way leads us to a sacred center.

A desire to stand on holy ground, to be in a place where the veil between heaven
and earth has grown thin, seems to be a deep human instinct. Mircea Eliade
wrote that 'every pilgrimage shrine is the archetype of the sacred center. In
a sacred place we may experience the transcendent, the timeless moment, a
universal God above the differences of religion and denomination.
Shirley de Boulay, *The Road to Canterbury,* 1994, pg.6

The ritual act of pilgrimage is ancient. Man has walked sacred
pathways to sites of magico-religious importance for millennia. It is
one of the few ritual practices common to mankind today. Pilgrimage
is imbued with a unique psychological appeal to humanity's a priori
spiritual needs. Sacred line walking, a highly dualistic, integrative
ritual, is characterized by solidarity and solitude, self-denial and self-
enhancement, and penance and rebirth. Ultimately, the pilgrimage
ritual leads to a higher celestial divide, and descends to an interior
realm through self-revelation and privation. Ancient man embraced
this ritual's dualism.

Ancient peoples traveled predesignated paths through natural settings, infused with sacro-religious, curative properties. These spiritual pathways aligned with star fields and were affiliated with astral phenomena that provided the faithful a rare opportunity to divest themselves of the commonplace and follow the course of universal rhythms, experiencing spiritual death and rebirth. Selected by sages and walked by the initiated, these sacred pathways formed the setting for the actualization of the corpus of early man's sacred beliefs. Pilgrims moved along these lines and pathways to sites whose spiritual reality surpassed their mere topographical features.

Early man was inextricably linked to Nature's sanctity. Rudolf Otto in his work *Das Heilige* elaborated on early man's ability to discern the sacred. Sacred trees and stones were not worshipped as such, but rather represented manifestations of sacred realities. Otto called these irruptions of sacrality *hierophanies*, moments when the sacred is revealed. Archaic man lived "among or in close proximity to consecrated objects." (Otto, 11) This sensitivity allowed him a higher plain of connectedness to natural cycles, a deeper sense of dependency on them, and perhaps a keener sense of urgency to Man's position in the  cosmos and how this found expression in his immediate terrestrial domain. Sacrality was revealed in the stones, trees and the stars.

Sacralized terrain and star fields formed Man's vision of the ancient pilgrimage structure. Sacred routes were terrestrial reflections of prominent star fields and provided Man with a physical connection to astral phenomena. Pathways and lines offered opportunities to divest oneself from the physical world. The physical exertion of walking in natural settings promoted an unfolding of self, and an insight into a perception of the divine. Ancient sky watchers based their ceremonies, social exchanges and food-gathering activities on the heavens, and found their sacred star fields replicated in sacred terrain. (Hadingham, *Early Man and the Cosmos*, 7)

Ritualized line walking through sacred venues provided the genesis for the historical pilgrimage. Walking a sacred pathway integrated the elements of movement and permanence as well as sacred venue and final destination. These contrasting components gave form to the line walking ritual. Movement along the pilgrimage route did not merely represent a course to be run, but rather a process whose very steps were sacred and whose directionality was spiritually purposeful. The physical setting of pilgrimage is the eternal constant that undergoes cyclical seasonal changes, yet is timeless, immobile and indispensable to the form and function of ritual pilgrimage.

The pilgrimage routes ran through sacred, cosmologically charged topography, which offered epiphanies to the pilgrim. Woodlands, streams, grottos, valleys and promontories were intrinsically sacred. The natural setting of the route transcended mere esthetics and became more than a road to a sanctified terminus. It was an integral component of the ancient line walking ritual. Ancient man conceived of the divine as not being housed in artificial structures, but incarnate in the terrain. Terrain was glorified and its presence ennobled. Destination was a necessary outcome of the line walking ritual, but shared importance with the actual route. The pathway was self-sustaining and self-validating. The sacred route promised fulfillment equal to that of the arrival.

The linear nature of *Ways* and sacred routes were by definition directional and led to sites of powerful sacrality. Burial grounds, panoramic overlooks of isolated sacred grounds, architectural constructs such as dolems, menhirs or ruins of monumental architecture, and repositories of sacred items figured in pilgrimage destinations. Sacred termini promised the walker personal transformation, spiritual ascendency, and contact with the divine. Ancient people would have identified the telluric and mystical preeminence of these termini.

Robert Hodum

The Function and Form of Pilgrimage
Reflection: The Way is transformative and universal.

The pilgrim leaves his home. He is ready to forgo his familiar horizon;
he extricates himself from habit, which so easily becomes routine
and servitude. He goes off to an 'elsewhere', an unusual and 'extra-ordinary',
place the other ... an opportunity for the person who goes out to the Other,
to return as 'another' person.
Francis Bourdeau, 'Pilgrimage, Eucharist, Reconciliation', *Lumen Vitae* 39
(1984): 401.

The ritual act of pilgrimage has a universal form and function independent of venues and particular religious or spiritual contexts. Walking pathways through sacred venues has an integrative function in the community of the faithful. The sacred routes and *Ways* invite pilgrims to recognize a common corpus of religious beliefs, share daily devotions, submit to personal sacrifices, pay reverence to a sacred topography, and endure the unforeseen travails of the trek. Arrival to a sacred terminus is but a part of the pilgrimage ritual.

Pilgrimage fosters uniformity in belief and ritual practice for disparate populations that share a common faith. The mutual devotion to sacred termini and a commiserate reverence for the pathway provide an integrative mechanism, which promotes social and religious cohesion. Shared ritual activity spans linguistic barriers and homogenizes multiple points of origin. The ritual act of pilgrimage reduces the economic and social diversity found among pilgrims. All participants share the vicissitudes of the walk, albeit to different degrees and extremes. The act of pilgrimage forges a bond of mutual sacrifice and privation among peoples of disparate origins, ethnicities, religions, and languages.

Incantations, mantras, spiritual reflections, votive offerings, hymns, and personal devotions affiliated with sacred points along pilgrimage routes are common activities for all who walk. Sacred stones, personal mementos, votive figurines and other sacrosanct objects are frequently placed along the pathway. The confluence of collective devotional activity, personal petitions, commonly shared ritual activity, guided by star fields and sacred topography, figure in the line walking ritual.

The ancient and universal function of pilgrimage is often lost to contemporary eyes that interpret the ritual as simply a metaphor for life; the trail and its sacrifices as the life experience, and the pilgrim as the universal traveler for humanity. This secularization of an inherently spiritual ritual undermines Man's a priori need for a terrestrial path to enlightenment and spiritual transcendence. The act of pilgrimage provides the individual with answers to profound, non-parochial and deeply personal, yet commonly shared concerns. The *Way* satisfies the spiritual quest and elevates our connection with the *Other,* while underscoring the spiritual commonalties of all participants.

Blood, Terrain and Stars
Reflection: The echo of footsteps runs deep along the Way.

The holy place is seen as a physical location where the membrane between this world and a reality beyond is especially thin, where a transcendent reality impinges on the immanent.
Martin Robinson, *Sacred Places, Pilgrim Paths*, HarperCollins Publishers, London: 1997, pg.2

Walking the length of a spiritual path to a site identified with extra-normal objects dates from early history. Understanding the act of ritual line walking as it relates to St. James and his Way requires an examination of Spain's ancient peoples and their practices. Ancient routes aligned with a directionality that followed the rising and setting sun, traversing northern Spain and funneling Neolithic hunters, Bronze Age travelers and countless faithful to sites of sacro-religious significance for many millennia. The Christian Way of St. James is the most recent manifestation of a long-standing practice of movement along sacred pathways in the north of Spain.

Ancient Man was very much at home in the north of Spain. The prehistoric populations of this region left an abundance of remains in numerous habitation sites. These artifacts and cave drawings may indicate a preoccupation with star fields, terrestrial migratory routes, and calendaric accounting. Incised bones dating back more than 30,000 years suggests that Cro-Magnon man may have kept records of lunar events. (Wilson, *Starseekers*,20) Alexander Marshack in his *Roots of Civilization* examined bone fragments from Paleolithic habitation sites and concluded that the intervals and regularity of the incised lines and notches on bones might have corresponded to lunar phases. Incisions appear to have been repeated every 14 to 15 days, a pattern which Marshack believed to have been a "lunar model" or "a tallying of an important celestial event." Anthony Aveni expanded on Marshack's observations and sketched the pattern formed by the incisions and punctures in the flat bone fragment. In his *Empires of Time* Aveni indicated that an accounting of lunar phases appeared to be incised on "a 30,000-year-old bone tablet from the Dorgone Valley of western France." The perforations are indeed deliberate and indicate abstract thinking and a fascination with the night sky.

Perhaps, the lineation of those dots and incisions corresponded to not only star fields, but also terrestrial pathways. Instead of a calendaric rendering, they could have been directional and indicated a ritual journey that was divided into blocks of days. Aveni observed that the dots were not randomly placed, but appeared to have a linear continuum which reveals a point of initiation and movement along a line to a terminus. This artifact may have been a hunting guide that indicated a sacred walk or route that was integral to the hunt. Notches that appear on the side of the bone might indicate the number of visits during the seasonal taking of food or the animals found in a given locale. The lineation of the punctures may speak of a path whose sacredness embodied in the life-giving activity of the hunt would have been clear to early hunters. (Aveni, *Empires of Time*, 67-70)

Neanderthal and Cro-Magnon dot drawings found in the caves of the Pyrenees and the Cantabrian Mountains, notches and incisions on bone tools and rudimentary instruments common to habitation sites of these early Peninsular populations, may also reflect an interest in the lineation of pathways. Given that the hunt and its killing grounds would be a constant concern for early man, these lines may represent an attempt to record locations of neighboring habitation sites or terrestrial hunting routes of migratory herds. There is a clear interest among these Pyrenean populations to align, order, record, and represent objects, events or locations with simple linear geometry. Although commonly interpreted as calendaric, these renderings might represent hunting routes associated with astral formations, possibly aligned with the prominent star field of the Milky Way. Evidence of annual gatherings of hunters in Pyrenean grottos in southern France and northern Spain indicate group movement along a mutually recognized and frequented pathway. These ancient travelers would have been guided by astrological alignments and tools to aid in navigation. Journeys of this length would initially require a guidance mechanism for a safe return to the group's point of origin. Not dissimilar to animal herds and flocks, early man would sight by terrain and stars.

Star fields and astral formations figure prominently in ritual activity of early man. Archaeo-astronomy contends that the origin of myths and rites as well as the construction of ancient monumental architecture are anchored to the skies. Star fields may have been initially directional and would later acquire a stronger cosmological charge as sighting and directionality ceded to the need to interpret and explain astral phenomena. Perhaps the artifacts with dot-lineation speak to the relationship of a terrestrial pathway and the stars that appeared above it.

Prominent star fields visible in the north of the Iberian Peninsula have figured in the ritual practices of the cultures and peoples of this region for millennia. The Milky Way, often called the *Camino de Santiago*, is conspicuious among the star fields of northern Spain. Its visibility and apparent east-west directionality make it an obvious candidate for inclusion in the cosmology of the early Cantabrian and Pyrenean populations and an integral part of the sacred line walking.

The migratory herds indigenous to this northern region of the Peninsula would have guided themselves by terrestrial fields of magnetism and astral formations. This directional mechanism is well documented manifesting itself in guidance systems of migratory birds and certain herds of game animals. Mammals and birds guide themselves by using a grid system of natural magnetic fields and sight trajectories using particular star formations that align with feeding and mating grounds found along the migratory route. Herds of migratory animals following the east-west directionality of the starfield ranged through the valleys and mountain passes of the Peninsula's northern region. The seasonal grazing and mating sites of the fauna coincided with a longitudinal directionality which may have reflected the starfield of the Milky Way and paralleled St. James' current pilgrimage route.

Ancient fauna of this region followed migratory routes that human populations would intuit as predictable hunting zones. Early hunters would have noted availability and frequency of game along these routes similarly anticipated migratory movement along the pathway. The predictability of a desirable food source allowed local populations to iterate the importance of the route and validate its inclusion in hunting venues, cave art murals, dot designs and, eventually, in cosmological systems and ritual. Hunters traveling east along migratory routes of game animals would sight their return home west, along prominent star fields. Pre-agricultural hunter societies sensed the sacrality of their surroundings. Their vision of the cosmos would later be connected to the terrain and the animals that they hunted and consumed. Their sacralized vision of cosmos and terrain was reflected in the star fields that aligned with killing zones and hunting routes.

The *Way* of St. James has been associated with the night sky of northern Spain. The Milky Way's river of light illuminated early man's hunting grounds. Dudley Young reveals in his *Origins of the Sacred* that primitive hunters revered the blood of the animal and believed it to be imbued with magical *pneuma* or spiritual, life-giving essence. (Young, *Origins of the Sacred*, 133) The ritualized killing and eating of the game taken along a prescribed route would tie consumption of the magical liquid with a specific topography. The sacred nature of the hunt and its game would charge the migratory pathway and its corresponding star field with a sacralized character. This correlation of the sacred with a predictable source of food, an observable astral phenomenon, and a route traversed by animal and hunter were the precursors to a ritualized venue. Movement through this sacralized milieu allowed ancient man to iterate the intimate connection between earth and sky, stone and stars.

Bronze Age peoples of this region continued to ascribe religious significance to the *Via Lactea*-aligned pathway. Pre-Christian monumental architecture, dolmens and menhirs, were constructed near the sacred Neolithic hunting routes over which shined the stars of the Milky Way. The high incidence of Bronze Age monolithic, stone architecture along the western half of the *Way* in Navarra and the Basque region speaks of the importance of this zone in the ancient hunt. The concentration of stone structures may recall a terminus point of hunting trips, a major proto-historic killing field or the burial site of hunters killed by game animals later commemorated by monumental architecture.

Guided by the same star fields and astral formations and connected by an *a priori* consciousness of the sacred dyad of blood and terrain, Bronze Age man would recognize the sacrality of the pathway and denote this with his architecture which continued to ascribe a sacred quality to terrain. Man's cognizance of the *Mysterium tremendum et fascinans* in the stars and fecundity of certain land found union in the north of Spain. Underlying this duality stands the blood-terrain dyad of primitive man. Terrestrial pathways led past monumental architecture whose locations embodied a greater non-physical reality. The sacralized sites bonded man to the fecundity of the terrestrial course. Food, blood, stars and terrain provided an integrative nexus that provided the groundwork for the future generations' connection with the route. Wilson observes that, "sacred sites seem to retain their character of holiness over centuries, even millennia." (Wilson, *Starseekers*, 30)

Oral histories would speak of peoples and their prior use of this sacred route. Joseph Campbell in his *Occidental Mythology* recounts the origin myths of the Irish people chronicled in the ancient "Book of Invasion", *Lebor Gabala*. (Campbell, *Occidental Mythology*, 297) According to this compendium of Irish lore, successive waves of pre-Celtic invaders, originating in the Mediterranean, crossed the Iberian Peninsula and entered Ireland. The shortest route would have been across the north of the Peninsula following an east-west trajectory. The *Fomorians*, a legendary race of demon pirates from Iberia settled in Ireland. Considered the descendants of Noah, these giants, and the *Firbolgs*, originally from Greece and builders of the megaliths, crossed over to the British Isles from the Iberian Peninsula. (Campbell, 300)

Partholan and his followers, new arrivals from the lands of Hispania, defeated the Formorian kings but succumbed to a plague.

The *Nemed*, seafarers with the same Iberian roots, encountered and subdued the Fomorians. All of these legendary invaders came from across the seas, located to the south of Ireland. Many scholars tie them to the shores of Hispania. If such ancient crossings occurred, the most feasible and expedient of maritime routes would have been a voyage that left from the northwest corner of contemporary Spain. Ancient Irish traditions speak of an east-west mythic journey of successive migrations of invaders and colonizers who originated in or crossed the north of the Iberian Peninsula. The *Book of Invasion* bares witness to ancient chroniclers' familiarity with this route, the feasibility of sea crossing of this nature and its proximity to their shores.

The accounts of these mythical travelers and invaders might be grounded in actual migrations of Iberian or Mediterranean populations that traveled across the north of Spain and over the waters of the Atlantic to points beyond. Generations of their descendants would have recognized the mythical and extra-normal quality of this terrain. They would have identified sites of heightened spirituality along this pathway that aligned with the highly visible Milky Way. Ultimately, successive generations of peoples found spiritual ascendance along these pathways which moved through sacred venues, aligned with the region's star fields.

A constant to the demographic, cultural, and religious diversity of the many successive populations were the route and the night sky. The star field's alignment and mystical affiliation with its terrestrial termini gave meaning to the ancient pathway. An amalgamation of cosmologies, integration and reinterpretation of mythic religious figures, adaptation of festal cycles, and sacred venues would produce a region of sacred activity whose use and relevance would be uninterrupted for thousands of generations.

The pilgrims of the Middle Ages walked a path whose ancient origins would have been unknown to them, and whose ritual antecedents would have been obscured. Invasion, conquest, colonization and cultural assimilation and racial miscegenation obscured the particulars of the ritual acts and their respective religions as well as the ancient originators of the ritual practice. The sacred pathway bridged millennia, diverse languages and numerous religious traditions.

The contemporary pilgrimage to Compostela is founded on an ancient ritualized expression of spirituality, associated with natural phenomena and indicative of an historical continuum largely unknown to the contemporary pilgrim. Thus, the *Way* of St. James, a terrestrial pathway to Christian spiritual renewal and enlightenment, had antecedents which dated back tens of thousand of years. The pathway spanned peoples and civilizations that either never knew of one another, or had such cursory knowledge of one another's lives that their existence became subliminal, mythic, and legendary rather than historical.

Ancient Man Walked Sacred Lines
Reflection: Focus on the land that surrounds you.

The cult of the holy place seems to have preceded any other form of reflection on the world; it was the axis for future cosmological speculation. The secret of its enduring success must surely be the dramatic simplicity with which it forces us to confront our need to root ourselves healthily and imaginatively in the past during our search for a spiritual centre of power.
Karen Armstrong, '*A Passion of Holy Places*',
The Sunday Times Magazine, April 15th, 1990, p. 32

The ancient ritual of line walking finds expression in contemporary pilgrimage. Some pathways reflect the animist nature of the original line walking rituals while others incorporate the act into a fuller, more current religious corpus and are recognized as contemporary acts of faith.

The pilgrimage ritual may be realized in different venues. The actual routes may have minimalist architecture that melds with the natural topography, monumental structures that contain relics, oracles or Inner Sanctums, or sacred architecture, which houses the pilgrim's pathway.

Ritual line-walking through Andean deserts and mountains, as well as medieval maze walking in some of Europe's Gothic Cathedrals are scenarios for pilgrimage which give insight into the diversity of the pilgrimage ritual.

Walking the Lines of Nazca
Reflection: Let the path's rises and turns quiet you.

The act of walking can still help to distil one's thoughts so that all the worries that obscure clarity and peace of mind can rise to the surface and be filtered away.
William Dalrymple, 'A Pilgrim's Progress ends', *The Spectator*, 22 June 1991, p. 14

The drawings on the Nazca plains in southern Peru are examples of pre-Colombian sacred pathways. Discovered in the 1920s when commercial airlines began to fly between Lima and Arequipa over the Nazca plain region, the lines have been extensively photographed and studied. A 150 ft. spider, llamas, lizards, a dog, a humming bird with a wing span of over 200 ft., an enormous monkey and a 600 ft. frigate bird are some of the several dozen animal and humanoid-like designs drawn on the desert surface. The unique designs were produced by one continuous line that initiates the figure and terminates without ever crossing itself. The majority of these figures appear on the northern section of the desert pampa overlooking the Ingenio Valley. Geometric designs and lines varying from single, perfectly straight trajectories to several meter-wide avenues bisect and criss-cross these figures. The Nazca animal and anthropomorphic figures date from an earlier period than the geometric designs and lines. They may also have been constructed by different cultures. Regardless of their stylistic differences and their cultural origins, their presence attests to an Andean line-walking ritual tradition thousands of years old.

Once considered to be an ancient astronomical compendium by Paul Kosok and Maria Reiche, pioneers in the study and preservation of the Nazca lines, the designs on the desert floor were interpreted as solstice and star markers that formed a gigantic calendar. However, Gerald Hawkins, an astronomer and lecturer at Boston University, in his *Early Man and the Cosmos* revealed that the incidence of alignment with significant astronomical phenomena, with some notable exceptions, proved to be slight and due in large part to chance. (Hawkins, 175)

Ethnographic studies by Tony Morrison in Bolivia and Johan Reinhard in northern Chile and the Bolivian highlands point to the vital, line-walking ritual life of Andean Indians. Reinhard indicates that the contemporary Aymara Indians of the Bolivian altiplano continue to make ritual pilgrimages along straight-line routes to rock shrines. Parallel ritual pilgrimage along lines in Bolivia and Chile lends credence to the interpretation of ritual line walking by the ancient peoples of Nazca. These rituals provide a more complete understanding of the line-walking traditions of the ancient people of this Andean region. (Hadingham, *In the Realm of the Mountain Gods*, 243)

Evan Hadingham in his *Realm of the Mountain Gods* focused his efforts in central and southern Peru. He reported ritualized line walking in Indian communities in present-day Peruvian communities. Hadingham concludes that ritual activity centered on line walking through sacred topography to shrines located along the ways spanned centuries of successive cultures and civilizations in central and southern Peru. In *Lines to the Mountain Gods* Hadingham observes:

"Ancient Peruvians developed a sense of sacred space which emphasized the relationship of the individual to the sacred forces in the landscape ... particularly the long lines that connected the solitary pilgrim to the distant hilltops." (268)

The monumental designs in the sandy plains of this plateau desert region are considered totemic representations of the Nazca culture. Drawings of fauna characteristic to the region's ecosystem and tied to the region's most precious commodity, water, were integral to the cosmology of the Nazca people. Like the streams and rivers, which flowed from the sacred mountains, the desert lines were seen as channels and arteries for the cosmic flow of water thus tying terrestrial routes to the prominent Milky Way star field. The canals, aqueducts and subterranean waterways built by the civilizations of this region mirrored these spiritual, symbolic designs on the desert floor.

These sacred images served multiple ritualistic needs, providing venues for group processions and treks for shamans and pilgrims. Gerald Hawkins reported in 1968 that numerous concentrations of pottery shards near the totemic figures indicated that votive offerings were customarily left at spiritually charged sites near the designs. Entrance and exit points in the desert figures allowed pilgrims to move around the designs performing personal devotions and leave offerings along a ritualized and prescribed sacred route. Figures etched in sandy, rocky soil on a flat dry plain were not visible from the ground and, thus, not likely to be admired as works of art. However, these sites were considered to be functional sites for ritualized, totemic, *ayllu*-based line walking.

The pre-Colombian architects of these totemic, mythic figures and assorted series of geometric designs chose an arid environment where sand designs would go undisturbed for centuries. Ancient artists turned over desert stones revealing a darker colored soil that highlighted the diagrams' lines. The swirling circles and maze designs offered sacred routes that were walked according to a festal or sacral calendar. Supernatural deities whose favors were sought and malevolent spirits who needed to be placated resided in these desert-pampa settings.

The Spanish chroniclers described Cuzco, the Inca capital, as being the source of 41 invisible paths that radiated out from the Sun Temple, *Coricancha*. These sacred lines called *ceques* connected *huacas*, holy shrines in the form of stone mounds or rock formations. Originally considered to be exclusively astronomical site lines tied to equinoxes, pertaining to the sun and the moon, closer study has revealed their alignment with sacred springs, fountains, hills, caves, tombs and legendary battlefields. (Hawkins, *Early Man and the Cosmos*, 171) Ceramic pottery shards have been found along these routes and are considered the remnants of votive offerings of line-walking pilgrims. Incan history tells of animal and occasional human sacrifices performed at these rock shrines. (Hadingham, *In the Realm of the Mountain Gods*, 232) In Cuzco, the ancient capital of the Incas, there were several astronomically significant ceque lines aligned with towers or pillars on the ridges of hills surrounding the ancient capital. (Hawkins, 173)

A similar line walking ritual continues to be practiced in contemporary Cuzco. A pilgrimage rite exists among the Indians of the altiplano city that involves following lines out from the capital to highland sites of cosmological importance. Today's pilgrims deposit stones, votive offerings of cigarettes, coca leaves and open cans of sardines to the spiritual forces located at *huacas* that are affiliated with sacred points along the trails. Stones, rock formations, rise, turns and dips in terrain, caverns, streams and arroyos are recognized as sacred sites and are visited along the *ceque*, a sacred ritualized pathway.

These *Ways* of the Pacific Peruvian desert were constructed for the purpose of a line walking ritual, incorporating *ceque*-like routes to revered *huaca* shrines. The similarity of the Nazca lines with the radiating *ceques* of Cuzco and the line-connected *cairns* of Bolivia dedicated to the *silus* spirit shrines indicate a common ritual of sacred line walking. The desert designs were not overwhelmingly calendaric, nor overtly astronomical, but rather symbolic, figurative and reflective of an Andean concept of religious architecture. Ritual line walking was part of an Andean world vision that integrated the terrestrial sphere with its topography-enshrined deities and spirits, a sacred, truculent environment and a star field seen as the source of all moisture. Andean pilgrimage helped mitigate scarcity of water and other ecological challenges, made incarnate the cosmological concept of a terrestrial domain imbued with divinity, and tied to the stars.

An astronomical component runs deep in the cosmology of these Andean peoples, and is clearly related to the line-walking rituals of the region. Although the original theory, which claimed the lines and figures of Nazca were astronomical sighting devices, aligned with significant star fields and astral phenomena has been questioned, there is a connection between Andean line walking ritual and the stars. The history of ancient sky watching in Peru has focused on the prominent star field of the Milky Way. Its east-west arch oriented the Quechua, providing them with cardinal directions that manifested themselves in Inca urban planning. The alignment of the urban plan of Cuzco is oriented towards the midpoint of the Milky Way. (Hadingham, 229) Hadingham clarifies:

"The Inca have developed a unified model for their universe
based on the Milky Way which not only unifies space and time,
but also regulates the cycles of moisture and fertility that sustain
life itself." (118)

Spanish chroniclers noted the importance of this constellation in
the cosmology of the Indians of the 17th century. The Incas considered
this continuous stream of light as a river from which all the moisture
for the stellar fields flowed. (Hadingham, 108) Gary Urton in *At the
Crossroads of the Earth and Sky*, a study of Misminay, an Indian
community outside of Cuzco, indicates that the community's festal
calendar is closely linked to the Milky Way and parallels very
closely the cosmology and astrology of the Incas of the 16th and 17th
centuries.

Interspaced among the brilliant constellation are starless-sections
or *dark clouds* that play a major role in the cosmology and myth of
the Andean people. These stretches of dark shapes are known as
the serpent, the toad, the llama and its baby, the Southern Cross,
the fox and the tinamou bird. The creatures form part of the life-
sustaining cycle and figure in seasonal changes, periods of abundance
and drought, earthquakes and floods, harvesting and other terrestrial
events. (Urton, *At The Crossroads of the Earth and Sky*, 110) All are
situated in and mythically tied to the *celestial river* of the Milky Way.
Thousands of miles away the stars of the Milky Way also formed the
celestial pathway along which walked the souls of pilgrims to the
tomb of Santiago de Compostela.

The figure of St. James introduced by the Spaniards during the
conquest of the Incan Empire found a place in post-Conquest Andean
cosmology. Known by the Quechua speaking peoples as Santiago the
Thunderer, St. James frequently appears in processions and religious
feasts alongside images of the Virgin and local regional deities.
The pantheon of ancient Andean deities included Apocatequil, the
god of lightning and Apu Illampu, the god of thunder. The pre-
Incan antecedents of these storm gods were described as warriors
armed with lightning bolts. Visages of similar deities matching
this description appear etched on the famous *Gateway to the Sun*
in Tiahuanaco, in woven tapestries and mummy wrappings from

Paracas and on desert slopes in Palpa, Peru. These ancient gods of thunder and lightning found a more contemporary namesake in Santiago *el Mataindios* during the Conquest of Incan Empire. The conquistadors' blazing cannons and flashing Toledian swords that accompanied the battlefield cry of *Santiago* during their military campaigns confirmed that the embodiment of the ancient storm gods would be found in the figure of Santiago the Thunderer. (Hadingham, *Lines to the Mountain Gods*, 249) One of the children of Lightning and Thunder, the *Boanerges* found his place in the New World.

Gothic Cathedrals and their *Ways of Jerusalem*
Reflection: You needn't leave home to do pilgrimage.

Pilgrimage is a spatial prayer ... Thus, in the Middle ages, a maze or labyrinth was frequently marked out on the floor of the cathedrals and served as a substitute for the pilgrimage to the Holy Land ... here ... we have a striking example of motion towards a goal, one of the essential requirements which define the very nature of the pilgrimage.
Anne Dumoulin, 'Towards a Psychological Understanding of the Pilgrim',
Lumen Vitae 32 (1997): 109

The act of pilgrimage became manifest in the very architecture of the Middle Ages. The Gothic cathedrals of Notre Dame in Chartres, Poittiers, Amiens, Reims and Saint-Omer reflect the overriding need to do pilgrimage. Their floors, adorned with a curious patchwork of geometric designs, mazes, and spirals, typically formed with black and white tiles, are situated in vestibules, near main altars or at side entrances. The geometric form had a ritual function for Christian parishioners of the Middle Ages. Those who could not commit to the rigors of pilgrimage or could not afford prolonged absence from home availed themselves of sacred routes on the cathedrals' floors. The architects who designed the floor mazes of many of the cathedrals in France, Italy, Portugal, England, and Spain understood the contemplative predilections of their contemporaries. Pilgrimage would truly be universal, yet local at the same time.

Ways of Jerusalem, the geometric floor designs that spiral and intertwine, afforded the faithful an opportunity to line-walk as part of their personal devotions or acts of penance. Entry into the maze or spiral, meditation, and self-discovery are common components of this line walking ritual. Intricate designs guide the pilgrim from an entrance point through the serpentine complex of lines to the epicenter of the labyrinth. The central core of the design represents the sacred terminus of this abbreviated pilgrimage route on the floor of the cathedral. These local pilgrimages provided ritualized pathways in a sacred venue. This option of local line walking was a convenient solution for the faint-hearted or less pious pilgrim offering pilgrimage in-loci. Ultimately, it served the Church's goal to desanctify the natural landscape and distance its doctrine from the animist beliefs associated with the topography of a pathway. The ritual act of pilgrimage with all of its integrative socio-religious functions remained intact.

A continuum of ritual pilgrimage spans the ages and is recorded in the designs and models of ancient, sacred pathways whose designs were etched on rock, carved in desert sands, layered in mounds of earth, patterned in mosaic and constructed in blocks of granite. Entering a sacred pathway and traversing a ritualized route that culminates in a core sanctuary figure in these cathedrals' floor mazes. The syncretic nature of religious art, gothic architecture and the ritual act of pilgrimage becomes manifest between the pre-Christian, line-walking traditions and emerging medieval religious practices.

Representations of ritualized spiral and maze line walking routes are depicted on rock petroglyphs in the Canary Islands, Spain, Italy, England, and in paintings of the Hopi Indians in the United States. Roman mosaics from Tunisia, Portugal, Spain and Italy depict pathways and, in some cases, spiral patterns identical to those found in Gothic cathedrals. The syncretism of the Gothic cathedral's *Ways of Jerusalem* with pre-Christian ritual line walking is striking. Movement along a sacred line to the core of an intricate design reflects a pilgrim's spiritual journey of divestiture from the physical world and discovery of the inner self and divinity.

Chapter 9
ANCIENT PEOPLE IN THE LAND OF SANTIAGO

Words behind Compostela
Reflection: Names speak to us of mysteries.

The Christian Celts were concerned about the issue of the sacred landscape and about good and evil places. Christian ascetics sought out places where heaven appeared to meet earth. Christian monuments were raised at traditional tribal burial centers. Cemeteries were boundary places – doorways from this material world into the spiritual world.
Philip Sheldrake, *Living Between Worlds*, (1995), p.30

The origin of the name of the legendary resting-place of St. James may be derived from various sources.[24] Legend maintains that the Celts who farmed this area called it *Liberum Donum* or *Libredon's wood*. Granted to farmers by Queen Lupa, it was here in the wooded rise where the lights and music led the 9th century hermit to the marble sepulcher called *arcis marmoricis*. *Libredon's village* would later be founded on the site of a sacred Celtic religious site. *Lumbres* or night torches marked the sacred Celtic locales and figured in their nocturnal religious activities.

---

[24] Alarcón notes that the St. James legend is multiple whose versions chronicle the movement of the saint's remains from Iria Flavia, to Noela, to Pico Sacro, over the mountain pass of La Oca and finally to Amaea, later known as Compostela.

Campus stella or star field may refer either to the Milky Way's star field or the votive luminaries which were traditionally placed around holy ground by the Celts. This practice survived into the Christian epoch and was secretly practiced by the Hispano-Romano populations into the 4th and 5th centuries AD. The votive torches characteristic of Celtic religious practice may have been an attempt to recreate the star field's luminescence on earth.

The peoples of Celtic-Galician stock worshipped Lugh, god of light, the namesake for the contemporary city of Lugo. Known as Lugh in Irish, Llew in Welsh and Lugus in Gaelic, Caesar referred to him as the Gaelic Mercury. Inscribed dedications to Lugoues and Lugoubus in Tarragona, Spain, were derived from this divinity of light and found expression in the names of prominent cities: Lugo, Spain, Lyons, France, London (*Lugdunum*) in England. The feasts of *Lugus* in Gaul and *Lughnasadh* in Ireland were celebrated in his honor on August 1st. Lugh, considered the supreme divinity, may have been derived from an ancient Indo European cult dedicated to *the one with a large hand and long arm* whose name appears to have been considered taboo. The long handed god dates back to the Bronze Age, and was given form in rock carvings and paintings from Sweden to the Punjab. Called Lugh Lámhfhadha or Lugh of the Long Arm or Long Hand in Ireland, and Lleu Llaw Gyffes in Welsh mythology, the Rigveda called the Hindu god, Savitar, *prthupani* 'of the large hand', this solar deity, whose outstretched hand represented the rays of the sun, controlled light and the passing of night and day. (Ellis, *The Druids*, 124-126)

Of the 69 Celtic deities, Lug was considered one of the most powerful and revered. His mythic persona varied: a magician-warrior dressed in brilliant, golden armor carrying a lethal sling and a magical javelin and at times appeared on the battlefield and helped his faithful in combat, a sorcerer who was well versed in *"the useful and decorative arts"* playing the harp, writing poetry, building houses, and forging iron. (Herm, *The Celts*, 154) He was associated with crafts and the manual arts. In Ireland he was known as *samildánach*, *"the handy one who could do things with his hands"*, a guild of cobblers in Asma, Tarragona, Spain inscribed a pre-Roman dedication to him, and ancient Swedes called the large handed god *the shoemaker*. (Ellis, 126)

Lugh may be identified with Wotan, "the great Shaman who hung on the tree of the world and died, and was resurrected as the Lord of fury, Wut, who was the magic heat that inspired Celt warriors. Possessing magical powers, he would ride into battle on horseback holding an infallible spear." (Herm, 156) The moon was worshipped on the coasts of Galicia; dances were celebrated during periods of full moon. Day and nocturnal light figured prominently in the symbology of the region. They used euphemisms when speaking of the divinities, given that speaking the names of their gods, most particularly the moon goddess, was taboo to. (Tuñón, *Historia de España: Primeras culturas*, 408) The Lugh cult was anchored firmly in the history of the region where the legendary history of St. James developed and Compostela now stands.

The origin of Compostela may be related to a series of ancient burial sites and the term Compostela would be derived from *Campus Stellae* that designated burial fields and tombs. There are several pre-Christian and Christian cemeteries found along the western route of the *Way* whose locale figure in the St. James legend and lore. The juxtaposing of ancient burial sites with towns and settlements prominent in the St. James history gives more insight into the etymology of St. James' resting-place. Compostela appears to have been one of several tombs, shrines and reliquaries recognized and used by pre-Christian and early Christian Gallaecians. The cemetery of Santa María of Iria Flavia may have been the repository of relics originating from southern Spain during the Moor's invasion of Muza in the early 700s. Once located in Padrón, a town steeped in St. James legend and lore, the church was renamed in honor of St. James. Located in the contemporary town of Noya the cemetery of Santa María de Nova is linked to the mythic city of *Noela* reportedly founded by a granddaughter of Noah. In Finisterre, site of the *Promotorium Celticum*, a destination of Gallaecian-Celtic pilgrimage lays the hallowed grounds of the cemetery of Santa María del Fin de la Tierra. (Alarcón, 61-62)

Compostela may derive from the presence of a Roman military camp and its war or road tower. It has been proposed that the name may simply refer to a site that was well built and strategically situated and, thus, *composte*, referring to a small, well designed camp.

Dolmens, Circles of Stone and Roman Sepulcrum
Reflection: The Way is a portal to the past.

The peregrinus is the foreigner, walking over the land of others,
seeking the Other.
Anne Dumoulin, "Towards a Psychological Understanding of the Pilgrim',
Lumen Vitae 32, 1977: 112-3

The northwestern region of Spain represents a multifaceted cultural panorama, bordering on the enigmatic. The migratory crossings and multiple settlements of this region complicate the ethno-cultural puzzle of Galicia. Long believed to be comprised of exclusively Celtic cultural units, there existed numerous cultural antecedents to the historic peoples encountered by the Romans in the first century BC. The people who inhabited and ultimately formed the ethno-cultural and cosmological background of pre-Roman Galicia were diverse. Recent findings and interpretations of the archaeological record of this region are incomplete and contradictory. The cultural mosaic revealed by the research speaks of a region densely inhabited in the early Bronze Age, subjected to migratory waves of proto-Indo European and Indo-European peoples, colonized by Romans and peopled by Germanic tribes.

The archaeology of the Amaea valley indicates a coexistence of Celtic and Roman populations dating from the first to the fourth centuries AD. The ancient urban plan of the Amaea valley included a Celtic settlement and community with a wooden stockade built on a rise in the valley. Other sources denote it as an ancient *compostum* or cemetery that predated the imperial town. The Celtic inhabitants of this region were known as the *capori* who ranged between Iria Flavia and Lucus Augusti. They like the other Celtic populations engaged in inter-Peninsular trade, worshipped divinities who were identified with the mountains and streams of the region, honored their war god, Cosus, worshipped the sun and the moon, practiced divination, cremated their dead and buried their ashes in funerary urns, took trophy heads in combat, and paid homage to the *lares viales*, gods and goddess who inhabited the roadways, thoroughfares and crossroads.

Recent archaeological excavations have revealed that the *Castreña Culture* specific to the northwestern region nearest San Fiz de Solovio and contemporary Compostela was likely the cultural group from which the inhabitants of the D'Amaía valley's castrum came. This cultural group was named after their settlements called *castros* or *citanías*. These circular stone homes surrounded by rock fortifications provided the nucleus for all social, cultural, and political activities of these people. Their *castros* included ovens for the cremation of their dead and circular, stone habitation sites. The racial stock appears to have been descended from the *saefe* people who in the 6th century BC settled along the Atlantic coast in this region. After initial warfare with the *oestriminians,* the archaeological record indicates a long, uninterrupted period of habitation from the 7th century to the 4th century AD. In *Historia de España: colonizaciones y formación de los pueblos preromanos 1200 - 218 BC.* Malquer de Motes traced a chronology which spanned ten centuries of *Castreña* occupation of this region up to and including three hundred years of coexistence with the Romans and a clear pattern of assimilation of Roman architectural design and urban planning and organization.[25] This period of contact characterized by Angel Montenegro indicates receptivity to Roman social organization and urban design.

The *Via Loca Maritima*, a Roman way, crossed the valley and connected the Roman castrum or military camp, located on a hillock near the Celtic community, with the rest of the Empire. The roadway, which headed up from the estuary port at Ulla supplied the settlements of Lucus Augusta in the north and Brigantium Augusta in the south.[26] Flanked by the Sar and Sarela Rivers, the outskirts of the ancient Celtic community of Amaea or Amaía had a Roman

---

[25] Castreño tardío (siglos II-I a. C.) Período de contacto con el mundo romano, aparecen nuevos patrones organizativos y edificios con funciones públicas. (506) Montenegro cites other authors who have replicated de Motes' findings and established a similar scheme, "Castreño IV: Pervivencia castreña en la cultura romana provincial, especialmente áreas rurales, con un intento de asimilar el nuevo tipo de urbanismo (siglos I - IV d.C.)"

[26] Iria Flavia is contemporary Padrón, Braccara Augusta is Braga, Farum Brigantium is Coruña, Conímbriga is Coimbra, Lucus Augusti is Lugo, Legio VII Gémina is León, Clunia is Coruña del Conde (Burgos) Cesar Augusta is Zaragoza, Emérita Augusta is Mérida. Of course, the ancient Gallaecia is contemporary Galicia.

presence by the 100 AD. The Roman camp formed the nucleus of the Christian dioceses of Iria Flavia. As the Roman garrison grew and the camp became a larger community, the Celtic castrum-settlement was absorbed, forming part of the outlying neighborhoods of the expanding town.

The remains of a Roman *sepulcra*, hot baths, the stone base of an observation tower, and a rock wall have been found under the original floor of the church, built by Alfonso II around 813 AD. An uninterrupted period of Roman habitation extends from the first century AD to the fourth. A second period of Roman remains date from the middle of the fourth to the fifth century AD. The Roman road, *via loca maritima,* passed immediately west of the fortified tower. Its remains have been found under the south west section of the present-day cathedral.

By the 9th century AD the local church authorities had erected a chapel dedicated to San Fiz de Solovio in the ancient Celtic town of Amaea or Amaía. The small basilica was located on the hilly ruins of a Celtic pagan sanctuary and ancient compostum or necropolis, situated southeast of a Roman camp. This small settlement would become the venue for the discovery of the tomb of Saint James.

This historic population known by the Romans as Gallaecians lived to the west of their neighbors the Austres and Cantabri and along the Navia River. The Gallicians, Austres and Cantabri peoples may have predated the arrival of pre-Celtic and Celtic migratory waves into the north by many centuries, inhabiting the Cantabrian mountain range and its valleys. (Montenegro, 229) These three tribal peoples appeared to have spoken a language derived from or including elements from an ancient Indo European source, far more ancient than the Celt Iberian language, common to the north and northeast of Spain. This language is most closely related to Atlantic coastal zones and may show a strong influence from the early Atlantic Bronze Age peoples, who significantly predated the arrival of the first Celts. (Tuñón, *Historia de España*, 162)

These three ethno-cultural entities shared a common castrum-based social structure in which each settlement enjoyed apparent political independence from the surrounding communities. The northwestern component of the Galician population was divided into two administrative counties or territories. According to Roman historians, the Bracarense territory in central and southwestern Galicia had twenty nine settlements or *castellum* with 285,000 tribute-paying men or free men. Bracara Augusta was its administrative center, situated in the southwest corner of Galicia. The Lucense territory had its administrative center in Lucus Agusti in the north with 16 castellum and 166,000 tribute-paying men. (163)

Settlements were situated on elevated ground enclosed by palisades, enjoyed relative political independence from the territories' capitals, maintained a thriving inter-castrum trade, and developed a metallurgy industry which exploited the rich mineral deposits of the northwest corner of the Peninsula. Galician commerce focusing on the flow of gold, cooper, tin, lead, and ceramics was conducted along Atlantic maritime and over-land trade routes with the Greeks, Phoenicians, as well as Indo European settlements in the south and the Mediterranean coast. They meet the Oestriminians, a proto-Indo European population that had arrived in this northwestern section of Spain in the 7th century BC. These ancient peoples initially encountered a megalithic Bronze Age cultural group.

An early Celtic population migrated to the west and settled in the northwestern corner of the Iberian Peninsula around the end of the 6th century BC. (Montenegro, *Historia de España*, 229) This early group of Celts had numerous similarities with the Celts of France, the British Isles, and other Celtic populations that already occupied the south-western lands of the Iberian Peninsula.[27] These populations were influenced by other cultural groups that they encountered during their migration. Settling in regions ranging from the Ebro Valley and the Cataluña region to the Atlantic coast of the Peninsula, they maintained a pronounced similarity in their religion, language, and their socio-economic structure. (Tuñón, 161)

The classic Celtic motifs of a warrior nobility, geometric adornments, and hierarchical social organization, indigenous to southern Spain, appear in the northwest. This Celtic group reflected

---

[27] Celtic peoples inhabited the extreme south of the Iberian Peninsula building turres, rectangular fortifications, and mining copper and salt around the middle of the 7th century BC. Settlements, situated along communication routes and elevated topography provided an advantage for defense, were based on communal habitation sites located near rivers.

the religious, economic, and social structures of Mediterranean peoples (Iberians, Greeks and Phoenicians) whose settlements they passed as they moved south through France, over the Pyrenees, down to the central plains of Castille, and along the Spanish Levant. (Montenegro, 226-227) The presence of the *cempsi* of the Guadiana region and the *celtici* from Extremadura, the *lusis* and *saephes* (safaes) from southern Castille, Extremadura and western Portugal appear in the ethno-cultural melting pot of the northwest. Their use of circular homes and metallurgy industry, coupled with a matrilineal-based kinship network, added a new cultural dimension to the northwest populations. (229)

This Celtic migration followed the arrival of the Lusitanians in Portugal in the early 6th century BC. The *tribe of Lusus* occupied both central and south western Portugal; not discounting a cursory movement into northwestern Spain. As they moved northward, the Lusitanians would eventually encounter the Gallaecians who inhabited the Cantabrian mountain region. It is believed that common linguistic and cultural similarities between the northwestern Celtic and Atlantic Lusitanian peoples may indicate a continuation of Lusitanian migrations into the Atlantic coast of the Iberian Peninsula, ranging up into the northwest of Spain. In fact, during ancient times, the Gallaecian Celts were called Lusitanians.

The Celtic-Lusitanian population was but one of several tribal-based groups and cultural overlays present in the Galician region of Spain. The northwestern corner of Spain appears to have been settled by subsequent waves of Celt-like people during the later part of the third century BC. (Montenegro, 501) This cultural group provided the final ethnic overlay of the already diverse Gallaecian cultural zone. First encountered by the Romans in 138 BC, the Celtic Gallaecians expanded territorially when Bruto *Décimo* led a military expedition to the Miño Valley. They were the most prominent and powerful of the indigenous populations and thus their tribal name became synonymous with the people of the entire region and its tribes. (501)

A significant Atlantic Bronze Age culture populated the Galician coast and its valleys and predated all of the peoples of the previously mentioned demographic movements. The ancient people found along the Atlantic coast and valleys, representatives of a megalithic Bronze Age culture that extended from the south of Portugal to the northern most tip of Galicia, date from 3,000 to 2,000 BC. This northwest Bronze Age population is closely related to the megalithic culture of Portugal whose cultural orientation was decidedly not Mediterranean. This strong pre-Indo European cultural zone reflected the Atlantic coastal groups of the British Isles and Brittany, but not the Mediterranean's ethno-cultural basin. These densely populated settlements had a close cultural affiliation with the non-Indo European settlements of the Duero Plateau and Valley. (Montenegro, *Historia de España*, 499 – 502) [28]

This dolmen-building, megalithic culture may have extended from the Iberian Peninsula, along the coast of southwestern France, and up into the British Isles. The exploitation of mineral resources and Bronze Age commerce, which sought out copper, tin, gold, silver and lead, may have forged a maritime link between the British Isles and the northwest of the Iberian Peninsula. (Tuñón, 75) Excavations indicate a very active center of foundries in Galicia, demonstrating a clear affinity with coastal Bronze Age cultures of France and the British Isles. (75) The metallurgy industry present in Galicia reflected the typology and designs of utensils and weapons found in Bronze Age Britain and France. (95) The existence of a complex Bronze Age culture in Galicia is clear and predates the arrival of even the earliest Celtic population. However, this unique culture would succumb to successive waves of Indo European peoples who settled in Spain starting in the first millennium BC.

Migratory movements of many cultural groups figured in the formation of the people the Romans identified as the Galicians. Upon the arrival of the Romans, this ethno-cultural group represented the descendants of pre-Indo European peoples, a megalithic Atlantic Bronze Age population, Greek-descended Ligurians from the Mediterranean coast, waves of Indo-European Celtic Saefe peoples, and tribes of the La Téne culture from the 3rd century BC. These cultures formed the cosmological substratum that intertwined and enriched the lore and legend of the region. It was at a Roman camp and a Celt-descended settlement, later called San Felix-Fiz de Solovio,

[28] Indicators of a migratory wave of pre-Indo-European, not specifically Celtic groups around 700 BC.

that the Santiago legendary history would be situated. Ancient lore and myth, pre-Christian cosmologies, and centuries of Christian tradition contributed to making this venue the mystical and enigmatic Compostela, site of pilgrimage for millions and the shrine for the patron saint of an emerging Spain.

The Germanic tribe, the Sueves, was last significant population to inhabit the northwestern corner of Spain. Braga was the bishopric of the Suevi population in the fifth century AD. The Sueves had formed an uneasy alliance with the Church, intermittently rejecting and accepting the Arian and Catholic forms of Christianity during their 179-year rule. Martin of Braga converted the Sueves shortly after his arrival to the region in 556 AD. The sudden expansion of the Suevi influence in Galicia ended when Leovigild and the Arian Goths destroyed the Suevi tribes in 585. (Ferreiro, 6) The Arian faith of the Goths was the final spiritual overlay before Roman Catholicism would consolidate its hegemony in the northwest corner of the Peninsula.

Chapter 10
THE WAY IN 21ˢᵗ CENTURY SPAIN

The Way Endures
Reflection: We face the future together.

We all go on pilgrimage. It is part of our human yearning to associate places
with people we love, with experiences, which are precious, with events, which
are holy, and such places may be imbued with sanctity renewing our dedication,
stimulating our devotion and imparting a sense of healing, holiness and peace.
Brother Ramon SSF, *The Heart of Prayer*, 1995, pp. 120-121

A study of the Spain of yesterday and today offers stark contrasts
in political systems and national social values and behavior. Spain's
national life since its War of Independence against the French in the
19ᵗʰ century has been characterized by manic swings in political
movements, economic bust and boom and a redefinition of what it
means to be Spanish in the face of growing, regional autonomous
movements.

The monarchy, considered to be complicit with the landed
elite and the military at the turn of the 20ᵗʰ century, returned from
exile and restored in 1947 by Franco, was credited with saving
Spain's nascent democracy on February 23, 1981. The Spanish
Church, once an apologist for the oligarchy, aligns itself with the

poor, the disenfranchised and regional autonomist movements. The demographic trend of rural flight characteristic of modern industrial Spain has succumbed to the current middle class' gentrification of abandoned villages and towns. Formerly outlawed, regional autonomy movements have representation in the local and national governments and figure prominently in the formulation of current national economic policy. Santiago and pilgrimage to his shrine have managed not only to survive all of these conflicting historical events, but also, as indicated by the most recent statistics, have thrived in the secular, popular culture of contemporary Spain.

Pilgrimage to Santiago de Compostela has endured Spain's myriad of social, political and ecclesiastic changes of the last two centuries. The flow of pilgrims along its many routes has waxed and waned reflecting national crisis, political conflicts, changing social attitudes and prevailing philosophical trends in the intellectual life of the Spanish nation. St. James' Way suffered the criticisms of Europe's humanist philosophers' of the 16th century and weathered the threats of obliteration at the hands of the 14,000 occupying British troops of Sir Francis Drake in 1589. The Way of St. James survived the neglect from abroad during the Reformation and the diminished popularity during the period of Spanish Illumination. St. James' tomb became an interesting yet anachronistic, cultural curiosity for the Generation of 1898 and a venue for a circumspect religious practice for writers of the Generation of 27.

Fifty two years before the Spanish Civil War, the Archbishop of Compostela, after excavations had discovered the remains of three individuals buried in front of the High Altar, declared that the relics were those of St. James and his disciples, Athanasius and Theodore. A papal commission investigated and determined that the relics were authentic.On November 2, 1884, Leo XIII proclaimed to the world the authenticity of the remains in his apostolic letter *Deus Omnipotens*, declaring their validity in perpetuum.

Compostela assumed the mantle of being the spiritual center of Spain when Franco rededicated it to the Nationalist cause of post-Civil War Spain. In post-war Europe Pope Pius XII underscored the importance of pilgrimage to Compostela. His pronouncement to the world in 1948 stated, "...if the pilgrimage had the noble function of consolidating the people's faith, of unifying the most divergent nations, of relieving the unfortunate and comforting all, surely amid the vast sorrows and sufferings of the present hour they will continue to be a blessing for the entire world." (Starkie, *Acta Ap. Sedis XL*, 1948. 414-417)

Currently, the pilgrimage to Compostela is enjoying a resurgence of national and international interest. The Holy Year of 1993 and its Feast Day of Saint James, July 25, were the focus of a significant upsurge of pilgrimage along the Camino Francés. Compostela's Old Testament namesake rivaled the icons and relics of Jerusalem and Rome. The ritual pilgrimage to the saint's tomb took center stage in that year's international ecclesiastic calendar and achieved notoriety at the secular level worldwide.

The socialist Spain of Felipe González and the Vatican of the conservative, critic of communism, John Paul II, combined efforts to promote the St. James' Jubilee Year of 1993. Local and regional government-sponsored celebrations, a national and international project of refurbishing hostels and residences along the route, the promotion of the Way's history and the enhancing of accessibility to the pilgrimage route by the Secretary General of Tourism of Spain figured prominently in the promotion of Santiago's pilgrimage. INPROTUR and M.T.T.C, a consortium of national and international travel agencies, facilitated the publishing of guidebooks, maps, devotional works and histories of St. James. The many Spanish chapters of the association of Friends of the Way of St. James, Amigos del Camino de Santiago, collaborated with local governments developing the infrastructure, which would meet the needs of the tens of thousands of pilgrims anticipated for the Jubilee Year of 1993.

The declaration of the Way as the first European Cultural Itinerary by the Council of Europe in 1993 further encouraged the use of the pilgrimage route. The Council acknowledged the unique, historic nature of the pilgrimage route by publishing a series of brief histories of St. James and his Way in various languages. They also financed and oversaw that signage marked the pilgrimage route from countries as distant as Scandinavia. The trails, which crossed the north of Spain, were reworked and clearly demarcated with signage indicating not only the pilgrim's route, but also the location of hostels and abbeys which offered a night's lodging as well as the availability of Red Cross stations, pharmacies and restaurants. UNESCO declared the city of Santiago de Compostela "Cultural Patrimony of Humanity" in the same year.

The first Holy Year in 2004 began the 21st century's celebration of 14 Holy Years dedicated to St. James. The opening of the Sacred Door of the Cathedral on the 31st of December of that year inaugurated the Compostellean Holy Year. Standing shoulder to shoulder in the Cathedral, crowded outside the Plaza de la Quintana, along the Ruas and gathered on the stairs overlooking the Monastery of San Paio de Antealtares assembled the pilgrim, the tourist, the curious and, as always, the skeptic. Jacob, son of Zebedee and Maria Salomé, martyred in 44 AD, honored and revered for over a millennium, will certainly not face the 21st century alone.

Santiago and Spain Move Forward
Reflection: Both friends and needs are met along the Way.

... for the end of the road is ever the object of the traveler's hopes and desires,
and thus, since we are travelers and pilgrims in the world, let us ever ponder on
the end of the road, that is of our life, for the end of our roadway is our home.
(Sancti Columbani Opera) Philip Sheldrake, *Living Between Worlds* (1995), p.61

The conflictive nature of Spanish history and its reoccurring theme of a people, who struggle, endure, adjust, and, ultimately, maintain a national consciousness, provide a keen insight into this Iberian people. The Spanish festal calendar figures prominently in a discussion of the foremost characteristics of contemporary, Spanish cultural life. Feast days and regional holidays are grounded in sacred namesakes; regional virgins, saints with religious processions and celebrations of the mass. Spaniards tacitly recognize that much of their festal calendar is centered on regional, religious figures, their exploits and extra normal events. To divorce the harvesting of grapes, quintos celebrations, and verbenas from the Virgin of August proves to be difficult even in the very secularized Spain of the 21st century. However, Spaniards only peripherally identify Spain as a Catholic nation and distance themselves from active practice of this faith. With a growing immigrant population, Spain looks itself in the mirror and does not see the past's cultural and ethnic homogeneity.

What is Spain and who is today's Spaniard? The assumption that the growing immigrant communities speak Spanish, share progressive European values and recognize if only tangentially Catholic cultural values is now in question. The Popular Party of José Maria Aznar formulated an answer to this question. The conservative elements of Spanish political landscape have invited their countrymen to reexamine what it means to be Spanish. Aznar's government proposed that Spain concentrate anew on its Catholic heritage, and invited the nation to reconsider the once commonly held assumptions and values drawn from a national Catholic identity. Catholic tradition, mores and basic tenets of Catholicism were promoted as being integral to the education of young Spaniards. Being Spanish from this perspective would not only be a secular, cultural experience, but one that is founded on a Catholic tradition.

Reaction to the Popular Party's apparent return to National Catholicism has been fiery. Parents of school-aged children themselves were reared during the time of cultural regeneration and national redefinition of the late seventies and eighties. The nascent democracy of post-Franco Spain abjured religious affiliation with the Catholic Church, welcomed the secular values of its northern European neighbors and embarked on the quickest course away from traditional Catholicism. Democracy allowed the Spanish people to entertain a new morality, enjoy freedom of expression and the right to opt not to practice a faith that had been endorsed by the nationalist state of the defunct dictator.

Political autonomy fomented regional identities through language, legislation and a curious cult dedicated to the new, exaggerated sense of self based on one's autonomous community. This celebration of the Comunidad, one's regional affiliation, was a clear historical imperative in preceding centuries when regional economies vied for hegemony and independence from Madrid. Today this social and cultural separateness borders on the anachronistic as we move into the 21st century. Interestingly enough, these regional autonomies are ameliorated by the figure, St. James of Compostela.

The pilgrimage to Compostela continues to be the most prominent and most commonly shared of Spain's rituals. Irrespective of regional language and dialect, city of origin or political affiliation, walking St. James' Way bridges generational, political and social divides in Spanish society. The voice of Felipe Gonzalez's socialist, liberal Spain has receded after the success of the traditionalist Popular Party. The economic well-being of the average Spaniard was bolstered by the euro, and loans from the European Union allowed for investment in national and regional infrastructure as well as urban development. Given the fiscal crisis racing across Europe, the precariousness of Spain's current economic health sharpens. But, the popularity of pilgrimage to Santiago de Compostela stands firm.

The average Spaniard's standard of living approaches the level of wealthier European countries. The imperatives of individual rights and self-expression in contemporary Spanish society have not wilted during the changing of the political guard. Peaceful governmental transitions are expected, opposition parties' resurgence considered a certainty, and the empowerment of the average citizen unequivocal. Spain moves most assuredly forward; some say careens towards its future with the same exuberance and abandon that young men in August flag down the town's fiery horned toro embolado. Live on the edge, use your wits and guile and firmly believe that you are part of a new reality, a New Spain.

All that glitters may not always be gold. Spain's luminescence has come at a cost. Most Spaniards recognize that change and progress are not unquestionably always good. The university radicals and rebels of the late seventies are today's parents. They now must confront the cultural onslaught that buffets their world. Recreational drug use has become an addiction. Sexual exploration and liberalization have culminated in higher divorce rates and a quiet but deadly AIDS epidemic. The cult of the self has begun the disintegration of the family. Free speech and self-expression have led to the loss of the subtleties of a language and disuse of proverbs, a vulgarization of common parlance. Regionalisms and folk wisdom that once were considered signs of rudimentary knowledge are unknown by much of Spain's youth. Technology has failed to foment cultural literacy. Nor has it supported a deeper understanding of the Spanish intellectual self. Language has become homogenized; quaint local dialects and witty regionalisms disappear along with the generation that fought the civil war. Through the pasotas, the okupas, the grungy urban insects of the ska movement, the litro and ecstasy Saturday night youth culture, blaring motor bikes, and, yes, Telepizza and Burger King, Spain moves inexorably forward.

And yet, there is considerable promise and enthusiasm in Spain. There is the celebration and reveling in daily life. Self-assurance has signaled the abandonment of the self-deprecating reflections of Fernando Díaz-Plaja in his El español y los siete pecados capitales. Mariano José Larra's classic, *Vuelva Ud. Mañana* has been consigned by contemporary Spain to a growing collection of appreciated, yet anachronistic historical essay about the Spanish psyche of yesteryear. Today's Spaniard has weathered threats to his democracy and saying no to OTAN (NATO). He faces the rise and fall of the value of the Euro, the growing economic crisis of the EU which impacts Spain, as well as Germany, France, Ireland or Greece. The streets of his cities fill with M-15 activists in the face of soaring unemployment as newspapers announce bank failures and consolidations. Aging politicians continue to embrace ideologies that a growing number of the Spanish public reject as ineffective and outdated. Zapatero of the POSE was voted out, and Rajoy, the conservative spokesman for the Partido Popular, rose to power. As the political pendulum swings, the euro falters. Austerity and salary freezes, bank closings and unemployment characterize Spanish life today.

Yet, he insists on returning to his village's ferias and celebrations, and revels in not only traveling internationally, but exploring the picturesque corners of his own country. Here, in the center of this vitality, cultural conflict and amalgamation, a swirl of xenophobia and anti-immigrant rhetoric, heightened consumerism and a growing fascination with cyberspace and scientific research stands St. James. Pilgrimage to Compostela continues to be practiced. Spain's most enduring national narrative is the legendary history of a Jew who was martyred in Judea, mythically transported to Rome's most distant and rebellious province and eventually named the patron saint of a country once considered to be Christendom's most fervent nation.

Pilgrimage to his legendary burial site survived battling Christians and Muslims, Norman raiders, invading English troops, critical, anti-clerical Spanish philosophers and a secularized society which holds the religiosity of pre-Civil War Spain anathema to the values of its popular culture. Santiago's pilgrimage has bridged the ethic and moral division between generations of Spaniards. The Nationalist regime highlighted Franco's annual visit to the saint's cathedral and extolled the virtues of Spain's post-war National Catholicism. St. James' pilgrimage has been promoted and financed by the Holy See, the conservative Partido Popular and the PSOE, Spain's socialist party aligned with the secular, materialistic cultural of contemporary Spain. Young and old, socialist and conservative, catholic, agnostic and esotericist, adventurer and curiosity seeker are drawn along the same path. Disparate motives are fused by a voice and presence whose invitation has been made to generations; Come and walk the Way. Many have listened and discovered the satisfaction found only in pilgrimage to the House of James. To unplug, disengage and quiet the noise of the 21st century's milieu. To walk along the path of stars the terrestrial Milky Way to the house of James and come to Compostela.

And so, we have made the acquaintance of Catholic Spain's St. James. Influenced by ascetic Essenes, he was cousin to Jesus and heir to the Davidic throne. St James the Greater most likely lies in a shallow tomb in Judea. But this is of little importance. More notably, it is what history, lore, and legend have made of him, forever reserving his place in the firmament and on this earthly plane.

This martyred Jew, icon of Reconquest Spain and the Spain of intolerance and expulsion, embodied the resurrection of the *Dioscuri* tradition of pagan Rome. An ascetic astrologer from the shores of Galilee became the confluence of ancient deities, peculiar proto-Christian beliefs, and Christianity's fervent desire to survive and, later, conquer. His pathway immortalized his fluid and metamorphic persona. Millions of pilgrims, whose sacrifice along the Way hallowed the venue, rubbed smooth the pillars of the naves of his cathedral as they prayed to him for intercession. St. James, symbol of Christian and secular Spain, international symbol of enlightenment for pilgrims from around the globe, stands firm in this the 21st century. Instead of an anachronistic ritual, his pilgrimage has become an integral part of contemporary Spain's national psyche. St. James' and his pilgrimage have endured. Spain's quintessential survivor is certainly Jacob bar Zebedee, Spain's beloved Santiago de Compostela, and his pilgrimage, its most enduring ritual.

POSTSCRIPT

Reflection: Time invites us to reconsider.
Does the road wind up-hill all the way? Yes, to the very end. Will the day's
journey take the whole long day?
From morn to night, my friend.
Christina Rossetti, 'Up Hill', in *Goblin Market, The Prince's Progress and Other*
Poems (1884), p.194

As I have noted, the overwhelming historical evidence points to
St. James' absence in Spain. The legendary history of St. James as
depicted in the oral and written regional histories and lore are not
necessarily corroborated by the historical record. However, there
is some credible evidence that does support what the Church has
maintained down through the centuries.

In July of 2007, I had access to the Cathedral's Archives and
studied the forensic records of the remains unearthed in the 19th
century. The excavation ordered by Archbishop Miguel Payá Rico,
1874-1886, sought to locate the tomb of St. James. After a number
of failed attempts, the lead archaeologists José Labín Cabello and
Antonio López Ferreiro located an ancient tomb in the confessional
area behind the Main Altar. The discovery of the burial site and the
accompanying remains occurred in January 1878.

The findings, although well-documented and highly informative, were undertaken at the behest of the archbishop during a period of declining interest in pilgrimage. The archbishop's motivation received more attention than the noteworthy discoveries of these investigators. Some considered the findings and conclusions of this investigative team to be a deliberate contrivance and at best a historical misinterpretation to foment interest in the patron saint.

However, these documents present evidence that suggests that there is a significant confluence between the actual archaeological records and St. James' legendary history. The two most intriguing questions focus on recent interpretations of the forensic evidence, a detailed study of the burial chamber and a recent photographic investigation of the grave site.

The discovery of the burial site and remains in January of 1878 shed light on the archaeology of the cathedral and the numerous burial sites under the main structure's floor. Several failed attempts at locating the tomb frustrated the archaeological team headed by José Lubín Cabello and Antonio López Ferreiro. The original excavations focused on the area immediately under and in front of the main altar. Although burial sites were located in this area, none approximated the appropriate time period.

On January 28th and 29th 1878 the remains were located in an area known as the Cardinals' Sacristy. Burial sites were found under the cathedral's center floor. However, there was one site that contained remains from the Roman epoch. The enclosure where the remains were found was made of brick and mortar characteristic of enclosures from the 16th century.

The burial site contained an urn that was smaller than expected for a repository for three individuals. Unfinished and placed in an inconspicuous location, the vessel seemed to indicate that burial was done quickly in an attempt to dissimulate its importance. No lapidary marked the grave. It was noted that the burial site contained many different types of human remains. Areas of the vault had collapsed, and bones appeared around the urn and the enclosure.

Finger prints were observed on the cement joints that held the blocks of the enclosure in place. No care had been taken to refine and smooth the joints between the bricks. The archaeological team noted the presence of wax on the walls of the urn's enclosure and wrappings. Could this have been the site where Archbishop San Clemente hid the relics from Sir Francis Drake in 1589? The disposition of the grave site and the urn, as well as the presence of candle wax, seemed to indicate a burial made in haste. A forensic analysis of the human remains would soon follow.

Professors from the University of Compostela formed the forensic team. The bones contained in the urn were not intact but were dated to the Roman period. The remains were divided into three groups of bones which belonged to three individuals. The first group contained 81 bones fragments, the second 85 and the last 90. There were over 365 bones in the enclosure and on top of the urn which did not belong to the three individuals. Some of these bones had belonged to two females.

The three sets of bones indicated an origin from the Roman period. All three groups belonged to males; two died in middle age and one survived until old age. No specific ages had been determined for these individuals. The skulls were not intact; however, significant skull fragments were present.

A skull fragment from Italy would help the team corroborate its conclusion that these were the remains of St. James and his two disciples. Archbishop Gelmírez had sent a relic which reportedly belonged to one of the disciples of St. James to Bishop Oton of Pistoria, Italy. The relic was returned to Santiago de Compostela and aided the team in the identification of the three individuals. The skull fragment fit one of the craniums perfectly.

A crypt dating back to the Roman period was also the focus of the archaeological investigation. The mausoleum was 6.41 meters long and 4.69 meters wide and stood less than 2 meters tall. It had two compartments or rooms. The larger room had an open entrance and contained an altar. The second smaller compartment was located under the larger room. Access to this burial chamber was located under the altar. No remains of a stairway were found.

The altar located in the upper chamber reportedly had an inscription in ancient Latin, which was dated to the Celtic era. Archbishop Gelmírez would later place a second altar over the original believing that St. James' disciples had erected the original in honor of their master. The inscription was copied and later removed. It stated that the burial site belonged to two women of royal and high standing, one a grandmother, the other, her granddaughter. The granddaughter predeceased the owner of the mausoleum. St. James' legendary history maintained that Queen Lupa converted to Christianity and offered her tomb for the burial of St. James' remains.

The lower chamber was divided into two burial areas. An area of distinction had been reserved for the remains of the younger female and those of the older female owner. A secondary area contained burial sites of three other male individuals. The burial niches were located along the eastern wall. One niche appeared to be more prominent than the other two burial enclosures. Two of the three enclosures had small openings. These perforations known as *fenestelle martiriales,* or martyr's windows, were frequently found in the cover stones of niches or burial enclosures of early Christian martyrs of the first and second centuries. By the 300s, the remains of the females were moved from their place of prominence and replaced by those of the male occupants. At the same time, a mosaic floor with motifs common to Christian burial sites in Jerusalem was installed.

In September of 1988 permission was granted to photograph the interior of the original burial site. Slides shot during this brief investigation revealed an intriguing inscription on one of the three niches. Near one of the *fenestelle martiriales* appear the words in Greek, "Atanasio, and martyr."

I offer these compelling facts to compliment and finalize my personal reflections on St. James. This is not the final historical evidence that dispels the doubts concerning the authenticity of the relics in the Cathedral's crypt. The historical record speaks for itself. The problem is that it tends to speak in different tongues, so many of which ring clear and authentic. It is ultimately a question of discernment, and for some, a matter of faith.

GLOSSARY

Abiathar - High Priest of the Sanhedrin, Abiathar encouraged his followers to apprehend James, the Greater, and deliver him to Herod Agrippa I.

Arca Marmárica/Marmórea/Arcos Marmóreos - According to popular tradition, the apostle's tomb, a marble burial chamber built by his two disciples Atanasio and Teodoro, was located here. The historic site appears to have been a small Roman temple or burial site, finished in marble. The entrance faced the west and the front of the structure pointed to the east. The term *Arca* typically designated the lintels of unearthed, megalithic dolmens.

Adon - Adon of France compiled a history of the early martyrs around 860 and mentioned the saint's presence and evangelistic activities in Spain and cited the existence of his shrine in Compostela.

Alfonso II the Chaste - King of Asturias (791-842) who sought Charlemagne's intercession in his struggle against the Moors. It was during his reign that the tomb of St. James was discovered. He was the sovereign who ordered the construction of the first church that housed the remains of St. James in 834. This walled settlement which measured 30,000 square meters became the ecclesiastic center of the region with convents, monasteries and the newly constructed residence of the bishop of Iria Flavia.

Alfonso III - King of Asturias (866-910) oversaw the construction of a basilica over the original church. Construction was completed in 899. In defense of the city against the threat of raiding Normans a second wall was constructed around the growing settlement.

Al Mansur (Almanzor) - Abú (Abí) Amir Muhammad ibn Abí, was the Muslim general who razed Compostela in 997. A skilled politician in the court of Hisham II, he rose to power through intrigue, favoritism and astute political maneuvering. He ordered the destruction of the cathedral Alfonso III had erected, but according to popular legend left the apostle's tomb untouched. History recounts that as he and his troops entered the cathedral they came upon a monk praying before the tomb of Santiago. So impressed by the monk's faith and fearlessness he forbade the destruction of the saint's crypt. This Benedictine monk is believed to have been Mezonzo, the future bishop of Compostela. Al Mansur ordered the removal and transport of the cathedrals doors and enormous bells on the backs of 4,000 Christian captives to his Madína al-Záhira, his new *shining palace* of Córdoba. He died unexpectedly in Medinaceli in 1002, according to popular lore, as a result of his blaspheming the cathedral.

Altars - Geological formations in Galicia have come to be known as Celtic stone altars, reportedly used for sacrifices, ritual activities and fertility rites.

Ambrosio de Morales - This theologian, citing local lore in his 16th century work, *Viaje santo,* placed the apostle in the hills of the Padrón Valley during the early years of his mission.

Ara Solis - These natural stone altars were used in the worship of the sun and located on the Atlantic coast of Galicia. The pilgrimage of the Celtic peoples to the coast culminated at these sites, once dedicated to the fertility cults of the Celtic populations in the region. Located in Fisterra / Finisterre, the end of *terra cognita* in antiquity, they face the expanse of the Atlantic Ocean and the setting sun.

Atanasio (*Anastasius*) and **Theodore (***Theodosius***)** - Atanasio and Theodore, St. James' most faithful disciples, figure prominently in St. James' lore. Some histories maintain that they stayed in Hispania and headed the bishopship of Zaragoza. Others indicate that they accompanied the apostle's body from Judea back to Galicia. Other accounts maintain that Theodore guarded the tomb and Atanasio remained in Zaragoza as archbishop. The most popular and frequently written history has St. James' disciples remaining as caretakers of the tomb whom upon their deaths were buried next to their master.

Azabache - Jet, a black marble-like stone, was fashioned by artisans in medieval Compostela into amulets, rosaries, pendants. Pilgrims acquired these amulets to protect against the evil eye and misfortune during their return trips home. When highly polished this stone was believed to possess magical powers and figured in a thriving stone industry, which began in the Compostela of the 13th century and reached its zenith in the 15th century. A brotherhood of jet artisans was formed in the 1400s. The Azabachería Façade of the north side of the cathedral bears the name of this stone. Indigenous to Asturias, Germany, Portugal and the Languedoc region of southern France, jet has been fashioned into amulets and religious symbols since the ancient Etruscans and Egyptians. Alchemists of the Middle Ages prized jet for its mystical qualities.

Baetica - This southern province of the Roman Empire in the Iberian Peninsula had two major urban centers, Hispalis and Italis, twin cities which straddled the Baetis River. The city of Sevilla and its river the Guadalquivir are their contemporary counterparts.

Beato of Liébana - His *Commentaries on the Apocalypse* indicates that James had evangelized and was *buried* in Roman Hispania. This Asturian prelate became the foremost promoter of the St. James presence in Hispania. He wrote hymns for King Maurcgato in 783 and 788 that implored James's intercession and extolled his saintly qualities.

Boanerges - Meaning *Sons of Thunder*, church history maintains that it is the name given to James and his brother John, the Evangelist, by Jesus to denote the intemperance of the two. It is also interpreted as a pre-Christian reference to Jupiter and his sons of thunder. It may have been a reference to one of the brotherhoods of the Essene community with which their parents, Zebedee and Maria Salomé were associated. This term may have referred to Zebedee who held a position of prestige and power in the Essene community, thus James and John would have been the *sons of thunder*.

Botafumeiro - The silver plated incense burner, used during the most prominent church holidays in honor of St. James, weighs approximately 53 kilos / 116 lbs. and stands 1.80 meters tall. The actual *botafumeiro* post-dates the Napoleonic occupation of Compostela in the 19th century. Eight men known as ***tiraboleiros***, pull on ropes connected to a pulley system which swings the incense burner to a height of 21 meters and reaches a maximum speed of 50 MPH.

Brath, invader from the isle of Eire - Brath, known as the son of Bilé, the god of death in Celtic mythology, reportedly embarked on the coasts of Galicia in hopes of conquering the Iberian Peninsula. It is believed that he descended from the sons of Milé of Inis Elga. Accounts maintain that he either arrived from the ocean to the west of the Iberian Peninsula or over the sea from the north. He renamed the abandoned city of Crunna, Brigantium which served as a city port for this Celtic colony.

Breogan - Breogan, son of Brath, rebuilt the tower of Hercules and discovered the power of a long abandoned magic mirror with which he contemplated the great western ocean and its maritime traffic. From Breogan's Tower, Ith, his son, saw the coastline of a distant isle. He asked and was given permission from Breogan to make an expedition to that land. Some local legends claim that Breogan and Ith recognized this land as that of their forbearers, Inis Elga or Eire. Legends recount that the mirror allowed Ith to see the valleys and hills, even the homes and cattle of the settlements on Eire. After deciding to conquer this land, he outfitted seven great ships and sailed out into the vast ocean and disappeared into the horizon.

Legend states that Ith was either betrayed and assassinated by the local Irish or that his ships were destroyed on route. Months passed without news of the expedition, until in the winter of that same year the body of Ith and many of his followers were washed ashore at the foot of the tower of Hercules. To avenge the death of his son, Breogan and his 36 chieftains returned to Ireland and subdued the natives of Tuatha De Dannan, as told in the Leabhar Gabhála, the Irish Book of Invasions.

Caprichos – These almond flavored cookies are sold throughout Santiago de Compostela.

Clavijo - According to popular history, the battle of Clavijo in 844 was the first reported intervention of St. James against the Moorish forces of Abd-er Rahman II. The saint appeared on a white steed, aided the troops of Ramiro I of Asturias and helped vanquish the Moors. The Christian king's refusal to comply with the annual tribute of 100 virgins imposed by caliph of Córdoba led to this military encounter south of Logroño.

Calixtus Codex - This manuscript of the 12th century is the first known work that describes in detail the pilgrimage to Compostela, the legendary history of St. James, the discovery of his tomb and the need to venerate the shrine. It narrates the appearances of James in Charlemagne's dreams, his call to the emperor to combat the Moors and to help establish and defend the pilgrimage route. Originally claimed to be the work of Pope Calixtus II, Aymcrid Picaud, a French priest, is recognized as the author of this influential work.

Compostela - The etymology of the term Compostela is subject to a myriad of interpretations. The Field of Stars, *Campus Stellae,* is the most widely cited making reference to the field of stars visible from Galicia, the Milky Way. *Campus Apostoli* refers to the field or resting place of the Apostle. *Composita ella* may refer to the small Roman settlement near one of the Celtic *castrums* as does the term *Compostitum*, an organized site or a small agricultural settlement called a *mansio*. This Roman outpost was located on the roadway Bracara August-Lucus Augusti-Asturica. The Celtic and Roman tombs and cemetery are noted in the term *Compostium Tellus. Compos Stellae* may mean instructor or guide to the stars.

Charlemagne - Charlemagne is introduced into the corpus of the St. James mythic narrative, lending further legitimacy to the nascent cult. Legend maintains that Charlemagne, after decisively defeating the Saracens, followed the star field of the Milky Way to Compostela in 814, a year before his death. The account holds that he donated the booty from his latest campaign to the basilica in Compostela. After arriving at the site, the emperor paid homage and continued to the Atlantic coast. Here, a mystery boat appeared to him, the very same craft that carried St. James from Joppa. Charlemane walked on the water out to the boat and was taken out to sea where he threw a spear into the abyss of the Atlantic Ocean.

Church of Saint Maria Salomé - Located on the Rúa Nova, this is the only church in all of Spain dedicated to the mother of St. James. Built in the 12ᵗʰ century at the request of Archbishop Gelmírez, this site houses the famous *Virgen de la Leche,* a statue that depicts Mary, breast feeding.

Corbuba - This Roman city in the south of the Peninsula is Spain's contemporary Córdoba. When Abd-er Rahman I rose to power and declared himself caliph, this city flourished and became not only the cultural, mercantile and political center of Al-Andaluz but a direct challenge to the rulers of Mecca, Damascus, Baghdad and Medina. Reported to have had the largest library of all of Europe in the 10th and 11th centuries, prestigious universities and over 300 public baths fed by aqueducts this center of the Caliphate of the Abd-er Rahman dynasty, developed into five distinct urban divisions with 28 neighborhoods with 3,000 mosques and a population that would reach 500,000. Córdoba declined and fell to the Christian forces of Ferdinand the III in 1236.

Costa da Morte - The treacherous western shores of Galicia are known as the Coast of the Dead.

Cruceiros - Built over pagan sites of worship, ancient fountains, wells and streams that were believed to be magical, these stone structures are comprised of stairs which lead to a stone terrace and stone crucifixes. Stone crosses are erected on these sites to sanctify dangerous ground where tragic deaths or pagan rituals took place.

Crunna - Crunna, the namesake of A Coruña, was reportedly one of the first settlers of the city founded by Hercules. It is recounted that Hercules took this woman as his wife and insisted that the city be named after her. Built less than two miles inland from his tower, Hercules' city thrived as a commercial port for trade between the northern islands of Britain, Ireland and Gaul, and the Phoenician city of Cadiz. Several generations later, his city was abandoned and the inhabitants moved farther inland. He named Hispalo, also know as Espan or Hispan, the first king of Crunna who was later succeeded by Hespero. The Greeks would call the Iberian Peninsula *Hesperia*, Land of Hespero, after Crunna's second king.

De Voragine - Jacobus de Voragine wrote the primary source for the St. James history, known as the *Aurea Legend* or the *Golden*

Legend, in the 13th century. Born between 1228 and 1230 in Varaggio on the Gulf coast of Genoa, he became a Dominican friar, rose in the hierarchy of the Order of Preachers, and was appointed archbishop of Genoa.

Dioscuris – These sacred human pairs, progeny of the gods or other divine humans figured in a sacred geometry centered on a triad. A divine male triad, composed of a central figure and two sacred earth representatives, created a triangular structure that supported the universe on terrestrial points on earth. Zebedee and his sons, James and John, may have been the last manifestation of this ancient phenomenon.

Dolmens - These megalithic structures found in the north of Spain are also called *mámoas* and testify to the presence of megalithic Bronze Age peoples in this region of the Iberian Peninsula. The dolmens' lintels once covered with earth are also known as *arca*, a term also used to describe the resting place of St. James.

Drake, Sir Francis - Considered a pirate by the Spanish authorities, this Vice Admiral unsuccessfully laid siege to *La Coruña*. Drake publicly threatened the relics housed in Compostela's cathedral in 1589. In reaction to these threats, the Archbishop San Clemente removed the relics hiding them so well that they were not rediscovered until 1879.

Espan and his magic mirror - Espan or Hispan, King of Crunna, built an observation tower on top of Hercules' original structure. A student of magic and esoterica Espan devised a mirror which could allow its owner to see great distances. He installed this mirror or magnifying glass on top of the observation tower which allowed the city's inhabitants to see approaching ships. The king was fascinated by the mirror's visions and carefully charted the comings and goings of fleets and commercial traffic. The economic well-being and safety of Crunna were assured as long as the mirror was used.

Espan and his brother Hespero fortified the city and increased its wealth in memory of Hercules and his wife, Crunna. However, with Espan's death, the port city declined, and the population moved away from the coast. The tower was abandoned and the mirror fell into disuse. Invasions went unforeseen and the coastal settlements fell to incursions from the armies of mercantile powers from the north. Local legend has it that during one of the Norman invasions in the 10th century, the invaders found the mirror and threw it onto the rocks at the foot of the ancient tower. Thus, all traces of this magical remnant of A Coruna's formative years disappeared.

Essene Community - This ascetic Jewish community's unique form of Judaism influenced many of the major figures of the New Testament, most particularly Zebedee and Salomé and their children, the brothers James and John. The Essenes were described as healers who had knowledge of ancient practices which included healing through the lying on of hands, and the therapeutic use of minerals, plants and stones. They were students of the stars and the planets. Their vision of the cosmos centered on a duality of a world of truth and righteousness, counterbalanced by evil and perversion, a world of Light and Darkness, kept in balance by celestial movement. Practitioners of astrology and students of astronomy, they believed that celestial movement affected the human condition and determined the extent to which this duality manifested itself in one's life.

Fernando II - This King of León (1157-1188) named Maestro Mateo, master builder, director of construction of the cathedral that stands today. Under Maestro Mateo's direction the cathedral was completed in 1211.

Finisterre / Fisterra - Know as the western most point of a pilgrimage route used by the pre-Christian populations of Galicia to worship the Sun God, this site faced the Sea of the Dead / *Mare Tremendum / Mare Tenebrosum.* It was here, according to Roman beliefs, the death of the sun occurred. During the Middle Ages, pilgrims continued to this point on the coast, following the path of the souls of the dead who journeyed to the waters of the Atlantic.

Gades (Gadir, Agadir) - This former Phoenician port city on the southwest Atlantic coast is Spain's contemporary Cádiz and one of the oldest and longest inhabited urban centers of Europe.

Gallaecia - This region in the northwest corner of the ancient Roman Empire is Spain's contemporary Galicia.

Gaita - The bag pipes of Galicia are regional folk instruments and may speak of cultural intercourse and flow from Galicia to the British Isles as echoed in these regions' lore and oral histories.

Gelmírez, (Xelmírez) Diego - This first archbishop of Compostela (1068-1140) greatly increased the political and economic power of this city. His concerted efforts increased the popularity of the shire of St. James as he oversaw the final stages of the cathedral's construction. Gelmírez crowned King Alfonso king of Galicia in Compostela's unfinished Cathedral. His military training in the court of Alfonso IV gave him the insight to build an armada to protect his city and its coastline from Viking attacks. Although embroiled in numerous political intrigues and the target of uprisings in Compostela, Gelmírez survived the rebellions and intrigues. He is remembered as the bishop who most contributed to construction of the monumental architecture of the city as well as its dominant role in Spain's Middle Ages.

Geryon - Geryon, the giant, was defeated and beheaded by Hercules. His head lies underneath the Lighthouse/Tower of Hercules in A Coruña. This mythic personage had the body of three men, fused together at the thighs and ribcages. Identified as the owner of a flock of red oxen, he ruled the island city-state of Erytheia or Tartessos. The Greek poet, Estesícoro of Himera wrote the poem *Geryoneis* in 590 BC that describes the encounter between Geryon and Hercules that took place outside of the Phoenician city of Gades, contemporary Cádiz. Archaeologists believe that this epic recounts the actual struggle between two cultures, the ancestors of the Tartesios, the *ligures*, and the pre-Phoenician population, the *tirsenos* or *cretenses* who might have come from the isle of Crete or Troy. Hercules, known as Melqart by the Phoenicians, defeated the proto-Tartessian ruler Geryon, whose city stood on the river delta of the Guadalquivir.

Godescalc / Gotescalco - The French cleric, Godescalc, the bishop of Le Puy, was identified as the first foreign clergy member to have made pilgrimage to Compostela in 951. His town Le Puy figured prominently in the pilgrimage route to Santiago de Compostela. Pilgrims during the 10th century left from Le Puy which was a focal point for pilgrimage for those either traveling to the Cathedral of Saint-Jacques, or coming to worship at Notre-Dame du Puy.

Known for its shrine of the Black Madonna since the High Middle Ages, Le Puy's historical role in the promotion of pilgrimage to Compostela had been unknown or ignorded until the 19th century. In 1866, Léopold Delisle, conservator at the National Library in Paris, rediscovered a manuscript of the 10th century that mentioned the journey by Bishop Godescalc of the village of Le Puy to Compostela in 951.

In 1951, the Semaine Religieuse of the diocese of Le Puy reproduced an article from the abbé Chanal, which highlighted the links between Spain and this French village. It cited the gifts that the kings of Aragon and Castile had given to Le Puy's Black Madonna, enumerated the Spanish shrines where the cult of the Virgin, and made reference to Notre-Dame du Puy. It was Godescalc, Bishop of Le Puy, who helped popularize the pilgrimage route to Compostela.

Golden Legend - This hagiography, written by Jacobus de Voragine, became one of the most famous works of the Middle Ages. It is a compendium of biographical information, popular lore, and widely accepted beliefs about the lives of the saints.

Hercules' Tower in A Coruña - The Tower of Hercules dates from the 1st century BC and was built by Cayo Servio Lupo as an offering to Mars, the God of War. Located less than 2 miles outside the city of A Coruña on a peninsula in Coruña Bay, the present structure stands 185 feet tall and is considered a Roman work dating from, or at least remodeled, during the reign of Trajan (AD 98–117). There is archeological evidence that it may have had Phoenician antecedents. A Roman plaque at its base announces,

Sacred to Mars Augustus
Gaio Sevio Lupo, architect from Aeminium, lusitanian, in a
promise fullfilled.
Aeminium is placed near the city of Coimbra, Portugal.

MARTI
AUG.SACR
C.SEVIVS
LUPUS
ARCHTECTUS
AEMINIENSIS
LVSITANVS.EX.VO

It was designed to be a lighthouse and watch tower for the important commercial port of Brigantium. It may have served as a Roman Imperial Custom House, regulating the trade of minerals and other products. A Coruña was known during Roman times as Farum or Farum Brigantium. The structure could date from a time when A Coruna connected Tartessos, a city-state located on the delta islands of the Baetis, the contemporary Guadalquivir River with distant regions in the north, Gaul and the British Isles. The actual Lighthouse or Tower of Heracles was rebuilt in 1791.

Hercules and his mythic battle with Geryon, the giant - Known as Heracles by the Greeks and Hercules by the Romans, his name was most likely Melqart, a Phoenician who traveled the Mediterranean basin, extending the commercial interests of the Phoenician city-states of Tyre, Sidon and Byblos. Melqart was asked by Phoenician emissaries from Iberia to vanquish a giant that plagued their land. The creature and his minions lived in the south and ranged across the land, pillaging, stealing cattle and horses, and enslaving the locals. He was known as Geryon, a ruler of a kingdom in southern Iberia and the owner of a great herd of red oxen. Hercules pursued Geryon and came upon him in the northwest of the Iberian Peninsula, today's Galicia.

The two combatants battled for three days, covering the landscape with flattened trees and staining the coastline red with their blood. On the fourth day of combat, Geryon lost his footing, slipped, and fell face down. Hercules quickly dispatched the giant with a blow to his head.

The victor buried the giant's head on Galicia's coast and commemorated his hard-fought victory by ordering the construction of a tower, the tallest man-made structure on the peninsula over the burial site of his foe. From that day forward, the Tower of Hercules, the Lighthouse of A Coruña, has protected seafarers in their journey along Galicia's coasts.

Hercules and his treasures - Hercules kept his many treasures in Toletum, contemporary Toledo, in a subterranean tunnel which ran under the River Tajo. Entrance to his treasure room could be found from the inner precincts of Toletum. Deep under the city ran a tunnel that ended in massive doors that only Hercules could single-handedly open. Written on the lintel, above the monumental door, was the message, whose Spanish translation appears below,

Rey Abrirás Estas Puertas Para Tu Mal.
(King, you open these doors at great peril.)

Each ruler of Toledo secured the door with more chains and successively larger locks until the arrival of Rodrigo I, who broke with tradition and opened the chamber. His lust for Florinda and ineffective kingship led to the invasion of the Christian kingdoms and, ultimately, the loss of Christian hegemony in the Iberian Peninsula.

Hermogenes – Hermogenes, a well-known magician, and his companion, Philetus, challenged the veracity of the teachings that James espoused. Philetus, as ordered by his magician master, confronted James, the Greater, and his disciples, asking the saint to deny the authenticity of the miraculous works of Jesus and his apostles. Philetus intended to denounce James before the Jews. The saint reasoned with his accuser, performed certain miracles in the name of the Savior, and converted the magician's emissary.

Philetus returned to Hermogenes and denounced the pagan's magic. Hermogenes cast a spell on his former disciple, immobilizing him with incantations. James became aware of his new disciple's fate and sent an emissary with a blessed cloak or "kerchief "to break the spell. The saint instructed the bearer of the garment to have Philetus say, "God raises those who have fallen. He frees those who are imprisoned. "

The Golden Legend provides a similar verse paralleling this account from Béleth, *"The Lord lifts up them that fall, and looses the captives."* Upon receiving the cloak and uttering the acclamation, Philetus was freed and fled to James.

Hermogenes, infuriated with the success of his rival, sent demons to capture and return Philetus and apprehend the apostle. Béleth recounts the use of a magic cloak that ensnares the evil spirits, sending them in pursuit of the pagan magician. *The Golden Legend* claims that the spirits were held back from the saint by burning chains fashioned by God. In both cases, the evil spirits were tamed and sent to ensnare the magician. Hermogenes, captured by his own creation, was bound and delivered to James. The prisoner repented, converted to Christianity, and sought protection from the vengeful spirits. James provided him with his walking stick or staff as a safeguard. Hermogenes offered to burn his many volumes of magical incantations. James, wary of the evil which might have been released by the bonfires, instructed his new disciple to throw the books into the sea.

Herod Agrippa I - Marcus Julius Agrippa, King of Iturea, Gaulanitis, Trachonitis, Galilee, and Perea, son of Aristolubus and grandson of Herod, the Great, ordered the execution of James, son of Zebedee in the year 44 AD. An Idumean, his family saw itself as Jewish and traced their descent through Isaac and Esau, not through Isaac and Jacob. Raised and educated in Rome, he was an intimate of Caligula and supporter of Claudius who appointed him King of Judea. This Romanized Jew pursued orthodox Jewish practice and policies and persecuted the nascent Jewish community which followed the teachings of Jesus. He ordered the execution of Jacob bar Zebedee and imprisoned Peter, the Apostle. Josephus described Agrippa's death by saying that he suffered heart and stomach pains and died suddenly in AD 44. Other sources indicate that he died *eaten by worms.*

Hispalis-Italica - Twin Roman cities in the south of the Iberian Peninsula are Spain's contemporary Sevilla.

Hispania Citerior / Ulterior - This major division of Roman provinces referred to upper and lower Hispania.

Hórreos - These squat, rectangular stone buildings, used to store grain and topped by a cross, are a characteristic regional structure of Galicia.

Ireland's connection with Galicia - Considered the claims of an exaggerated Galician regionalism, Galicia's connection to Ireland was initially given little credence. However, in-depth linguistic studies and commonalities of regional mythologies, ancient nautical histories, and recent archeological investigations support their historical maritime intercourse. It is now believed that the cultural, commercial and ethnic exchanges between Galicia and the isle of Eire were ancient and longstanding. Communication by sea between these sites has been traced to prehistoric times. The histories of both countries, Galiza and Éire, speak of crossings of the sea from A Coruña to Cork in ancient times.

Sea routes between the northwest of the Iberian Peninsula and the isles of Éire were a reality after the 6th century BC when Galicia and Éire were populated by Celtic tribes. Many feel that these peoples who lived near what is known as the Celtic sea, a region extending from the Galician Fisterra to the Breizh Finistère to the Known Lands End and to South Éire, had contacts by sea in pre-historic times. The strong westerly winds blew ships out into the Atlantic from Galicia and would have aided maritime activity.

The terms *galego* and *Galiza* came from the term, *old woman* in Gaelic, and may speak of a mother culture which found expression in the mother goddess *Caillaech*. In two altars in Sobreira, close to Porto, the name of the mother-goddess also known as the bone goddess reads *Calaicia*. The historical Gallaecia was home to a Celtic tribe known as the worshipers of Caillaech. The etymology of Galicia reportedly comes from the first Latin name for the area, *Cal-leac-ia*, and the name of the people, the *Cal-laec-i*. Galego could refer to the sons of the mother goddess, and Galiza "the land of the Mother-goddess" of the Gaelic Celts of the Iberian Peninsula.

A common artistic motif among these cultures finds expression in the many petroglyphs in the forms of spirals and circles incised on stones along the Atlantic coasts of Galicia, Brittany, Scotland, and Ireland. Circles bearing Celtic crosses or dots in the center, concentric circle designs and spirals with lines radiating out or into the center of this frequently used geometric form have been found in Galicia.

Inventio – This term denotes the discovery of a tomb and/or relics by miraculous intervention. The phenomena may manifest in the form of inexplicable signs or occurrences. In the case of St. James, witnesses reported mysterious lights, divine music, and celestial events that involved stars that hovered over the site that housed the saint's remains.

Jacques - These stonecutters and artisans built many of the religious structures along the Way of St. James. Their seals in the form of carved circular signs and letters appear in the columns of the Cathedral of Santiago de Compostela.

Jakobsland - This was the term used during the Middle Ages by Europeans when they referred to the Iberian Peninsula, referring to the land of Jacobus, St. James.

James the Greater - Jacob bar Zebedee, known as Santiago de Compostela by the Spanish-speaking world, was the son of Zebedee and Maria Helena Salomé, martyred in Jerusalem at the order of Herod Agrippa I, and reportedly buried in the Cathedral of Compostela, Galicia, in Spain. Jacob bar Zebedee and his brother John, later known as the Evangelist, lived in a crowded community of over ten thousand located on the shore of one of the nine *beth-saida* or fisher-home townships. His father, Zebedee, and mother, Mary Helena (Herena) Salomé, a cousin of Mary, mother of Jesus, like many Jews of their time, named their first son after Jacob, the ancestor of the Israelites. James, a seaman, fished the waters of the Sea of Galilee with his brother, John, and his cousins Peter and Andrew. Scripture inextricably linked James to his brother. Popular accounts state that they were inseparable. The brothers Zebedee left their parents and became the first followers of Jesus. James, identified as one of Jesus' favorite apostles in the New Testament, attended the reviving of the dead daughter of Jarius, personally witnessed the transfiguration of Jesus on the Mount Tabor, and accompanied Christ in the Garden of Gethsemane. Traditional sources note that James and his brother were known to be tempestuous, hence their epithet, *Boanerges,* interpreted by Mark as "sons of thunder ". *Butler's Lives of the Saints* interprets this phrase, as do numerous other traditional sources, as reflecting their "impetuous spirit and fiery tempers". His family very possibly belonged to or was influenced by the Nazorean or Nazarene sect of the Essenes. Jacob likely adopted the beliefs of his parents.

James, the Lesser (Younger) - Called by Mark *ho mikros*, "the runt" or "the small one" James, the *Lesser*, bishop of the Jerusalem Church, co-headed the Council of Jerusalem in 50 AD. A relic of St. James, the *Lesser* is kept in the *Capilla de las Relíquias* (Chapel of the Relics) of Santiago de Compostela's cathedral. In some quarters he is recognized as the brother of Jesus.

John the Evangelist - The brother of James was given access to the trial of Jesus, reportedly witnessed the crucifixion of Jesus, and comforted Mary at the foot of the cross.

John Paul II - The first pope who visited the city in 1982, John Paul II returned in 1989. A plaque commemorating his visit is located in the vestibule of the tomb of St. James.

John XXIII - Before becoming pope, he visited the city in 1908 journeying by foot and returned in 1954.

Josias - This scribe who led the saint by a rope tied around his throat, converted, refused to denounce his newly acquired faith, and was martyred with James.

Jubilee Year - The Jubilee Year is celebrated when the St. James' feast day, July 25, falls on a Sunday. The original feast day was celebrated on the 25th of March; however the Church changed the date to the 25th of July citing popular history as the date when Pelagio, the hermit in 813, led Teodomiro, the bishop of Iria Flavia, to the tomb. Pope Calixto instituted the Jubilee Year in 1122 and Pope Alexander III made the Jubilee a permanent tradition with his papal bull Regis Aeterna in 1179. The first Jubilee Year was celebrated in 1182. The Jubilee Year offers plenary indulgences for the faithful who visit the cathedral during that year, enter through the la Puerta del Perdón, say a prayer, repent, and receive the sacraments of Confession and the Eucharist. The periodicity of the Jubilee Year follows a distinct pattern, falling every 6, 5, 6 and 11 years. In 1122, Pope Calixtus II granted a plenary indulgence to visitors to the saint's shrine in each year that the saint's day fell on a Sunday. The Papal Bull of 1179 of Alexander III, considered by some to be a forgery, was believed to be the first confirmation of this practice. However, the earliest Holy Year appears to have been in 1395, although earlier documents indicate the existence of indulgences dating from the 13th century. The plenary indulgence is granted to pilgrims who visit Compostela during the Holy Year. This religious privilege appears to be dated from 1179 when Pope Alexander III in Regis aeterni confirmed the earlier Papal Bull of Pope Calixto II, (1118-1124.) It is now believed that the earliest indulgences were granted in the 13th century.

The Jubilee Indulgence is independent of the *Compostela* and may be gained by any means of travel to Compostela, visit the tomb and pray, receive confession and communion, attend a religious service in the Cathedral either privately or as part of a group and read a prayer to the Apostle on behalf of the group.

La Compostela - The official certificate is obtained when the pilgrim maintains an officially issued document, *la credencial* or *el carnet del peregrino*. This document is stamped at predesignated sites by clerics and secular authorities along the route. Thus, the bearer acquires proof of having walked the last 100 km. and cyclists the last 200 km. in one journey. The Holy Year of 1993 promised a plenary indulgence to the pilgrim who visited the Cathedral of Compostela, prayed a special devotion or attended mass at the site of the saint's tomb, received the sacrament of penance 15 days before or after completing the pilgrimage, and took Communion at the culmination of their walk. Originally named the *auténtica*, this hand-written and sealed document contained evidence of confessions and communions received by the bearer during the pilgrimage. By the 18th century, these components of certification were removed from what is now known as the *Compostela*. The *credencial* or Pilgrim Report, a document issued by cathedral authorities in Santiago and made available to bona fide pilgrims at different points along the route, churches and refugios, indicates that the bearer is undertaking the pilgrimage for spiritual reasons and has an open and searching mind. Access to *refugios* is restricted to those who carry this document. Two stamps per day are required for pilgrims starting in Galicia.

Leon XIII - With the discovery in 1879 of the remains of three skeletons by Antonio López Ferreiro, the papacy took the opportunity to announce the authenticity of the rediscovery. The Pope attempted to quiet the persistent rumors that the relics in the cathedral were those of the heretic Priscillian. His papal bull *Deus Omnipotens* of the 19th century identified the remains as being those of St. James and his two disciples. Rumors continued, claiming that the decapitated body had been buried with two others, one of whom was a woman, Prócula, the wife of Priscillian.

Libredón - This forested area located in the ancient parish of Iria Flavia, Libredón was the site where the tomb of St. James was reportedly discovered. Considered to be a magical place by the Celts and used as a burial ground by the Romans, the appearance of lights in the woods of this area marked the tomb of the apostle. The urban center of Santiago de Compostela stands on this site today.

The Limia River - During the campaigns to conquer northwestern Iberia, the Roman armies had to contend with not only ferocious resistance, but also struggle with the weight of myth and legend. The Roman legions that battled in the northwest of the Iberian Peninsula believed that the River Limia was the mythic River of Oblivion. *Lethes, Oblivionis Flumen,* the River of Forgetfulness in Hades, caused those who came in contact with its waters to forget their former existence.

By the year 133 BC, the western and central regions of the Peninsula had been pacified. However, the Galaicos, Astures and Cántabros of the north and the northwest continued to resist the Roman occupiers and lived as they had in ancient times. This region's mountains, forests, and deep valleys hindered the conquest of these areas. Perhaps Roman myth and lore was enlivened by the mist enshrouded topography, and briefly gave the indigenous armies an effective, psychological edge over the Imperial military machine.

In 137 BC, Décimo Xunio Bruto's campaign advanced across the Rivers Tajo and Duero, moving north until he approached the Limia River in Gallaecia. His troops refused to cross in fear of loosing their memories. Xunio Bruto dared to cross the river and from the shores on the opposite called out the names of his centurions, convincing his troops that the waters of the Limia were like those of the Tajo and Duero. He proceeded northwest to the River Miño, completing the pacification of this region. Accounts of the Galician campaigns end with his encounter with the Atlantic Ocean. Horrified and humbled by the sight of the sun sinking into the expanse of the western ocean, he abandoned his conquests and returned home.

Lupa - A powerful Celtic or Austre queen, Loba or Lupa, Queen of Wolves, received St. James' two disciples as they transported the remains of the apostle. The queen, uneasy with the foreigners and fearful of their magic, requested that they seek an audience with Régulo, the High Priest of the Ara Solis. Impressed with the powers of the Christian holy man, she ordered that her soldiers retrieve the remains of the saint and bring them to her palace. Astonished by the disciples' tenacity and the saint's powers, Queen Lupa converted to Christianity and offered her palace as a burial place for James. She appeared again in the legend in a postscript, which credits her with offering to destroy the pagan temple of the Arca Solis.

Bishop Maeloc - Fleeing the invading Anglos and Saxons, a group of Christian Celts under the leadership of Bishop Maeloc fled the advancing armies and landed on the northern coast of Galicia. Maeloc established a colony of British Celts in the 6th century AD in the land of the Sueves. These displaced Britons founded a see called Britonia / Bretoña. Accounts maintain that Bishop Maeloc was present in the Council of Braga (561-572) and represented the diocese of Bretoña (Britonia) located in the outskirts of contemporary Lugo. His diocese may have figured in the conversion of the Sueves who by 650 had converted to Christianity.

Main Altar - The ornate altar of the cathedral houses the three representations of St. James; Santiago the Moor slayer (*Santiago el Matamoros*), St. James, the Pilgrim, and the Seated St. James. On the sides of the bronze pulpits, stand the statues of St. John, the Evangelist, brother of James, and María Salomé, their mother.

Master Mateo (*Maestro Mateo*) - This master stonecutter and artisan directed the construction and completion of the current cathedral. A citizen of Lugo, he was chosen by Fernando II in 1168 to direct the construction of Compostela's cathedral. His likeness kneels facing the main altar. This figure of Maestro Mateo called the *Santo dos Croques* was carved at the request of Fernando II who was offended by his master architect's audacity for having portrayed himself among the apostles and saints of the *Pórtico de la Gloria*. The king required the removal of his image from the entrance's portico.

Local lore maintains that students of the 18th century began the tradition of touching their foreheads to his before final exams in hopes of obtaining his wisdom, knowledge, and humility. This is known as the *dos croques* or two light blows to the head. Local tradition holds that women who wish to be more fertile rub their stomachs and loins against his countenance. The statue is also called el *Santo de los Berberechos*, Saint of the Cockles, due to the figures hairstyle that imitates the swirl of the cockleshell.

Marian cult - St. James' Marian visions form an important part of his legendary travels through Roman Spain. The Virgin Mary appeared to St. James twice according to his legendary history. She interceded to spur on the apostle as he traveled through Hispania, attempting to evangelize the indigenous tribes of the region. Her first appearance occurred in Muxía where she rode ashore in a boat carved from stone. Her second and final appearance was in Zaragoza where she descended on a stone column and asked the apostle to build her a church on the shores of the Ebro River.

Bishop Mezonzo - A Benedictine monk and later bishop of Santiago, Mezonzo figured in the protection of the saint's relics and the cathedral's treasure. Accounts state that he fled the city limits with Cathedral's valuables before the arrival of al Manzur. Other local lore identify him as the monk who al Manzur found kneeling before the crypt of St. James. The Muslim general ordered that the monk be protected and the crypt untouched because of Mezonzo's piety and bravery.

Milky Way - The star field clearly visible from the north of Spain figured into the cosmology of the indigenous tribes of the northern Iberian Peninsula as well as in the legendary history of St. James. Known during the early Middle Ages as the Camino de Santiago, many believed it to be the *Way of the Souls.* Some maintained that the star field was formed from the souls of those who had not done pilgrimage to Compostela. Others considered the myriad of stars to be the souls of pilgrims who died during the journey along the *Way.*

Miriam - Mary Helena Salomé possessed the title of *Miriam* or *Mary,* a priestess who officiated at ceremonies and led the women of the Therapeutate Essene Community. These women of the Order of Miriam would have worn the red robe that signified *knowledge of hidden truths,* and actively healed and taught according to the Nazarene tradition of the Essene sect.

Mount Medulio - The history of conquest and invasion is replete with tragic mass suicides. Masada is perhaps the most famous of all tragic tales of resistance. The Iberian Peninsula has its own stories of defenders taking their lives as Roman or Carthaginian troops stormed the battlements of rebellious cities. Mount Medulio is Galicia's Masada. Site of the tragic and final resistance by local tribes against the Roman legions of Augusto (29-19 AC), Mount Medulio's place in history is assured by the chronicles of ancient scribes. Entrenched on Mount Medulio, local warriors resisted the Roman legions who laid siege to the mountain's fortifications. The initial attempts to take the stronghold failed. Standard Imperial tactics were followed; isolate and starve out the defenders and their families. Faced with death or enslavement, they preferred to end their own lives by fire, sword, and poison. The heroic struggle at Mount Medulio was not dissimilar to the final chapters of the resistance of Numantia against invading Roman legions and that of Sagunto during the Carthaginian invasion led by Hamil Barca and his son Hannibal.

Moving / oscillating stones of Galicia - These large boulders located along the coastline are subject to the movement of waves, strong winds, and the insistent pushes of tourists. The stones in Celtic lore made barren women fertile and determined the virginity of brides-to-be. During early Christian times, it was believed that the stones remained stationary for only the holy and pure of heart. The stone, *Pedra de Abalar,* reportedly can be used to predict the future. *Pedra dos Cadrís* is believed to have curative properties.

Mozarabic Rite - Mozarabic hymns, prayers and variations of the mass peculiar to the Christianity of the Peninsula formed a rite of longer duration than that of the traditional Roman mass. The rite addressed the Virgin Mary directly in prayer, used ashes during the liturgical celebrations of the Church, and required numerous responsories not part of the traditional mass between the celebrant and the congregants.

Muñiz, Pedro - Archbishop of Compostela from 1205-1224, who practiced alchemy and was an esotericist master, reportedly flew magically from Rome to Santiago one Christmas Eve to attend mass in Compostela's cathedral. He was buried in the central knave of the cathedral near the *Pórtico de la Gloria.*

Musa ibn Nusair - The conqueror of Morocco, Tangier and Ceuta, the last vestige of Roman authority in North Africa, Musa ibn Nusair organized the invasion of the Iberian Peninsula. Seeing weakness in the social and political order of the Christian kingdoms to the north, he ordered an expeditionary force to determine if the rumors of dissention and weaknesses were accurate.

Muxía - Located on the Atlantic coast, this small hamlet figures in the legendary history of St. James. It was here that the Virgen Mary's boat landed during her appearance to St. James. The large stone block measuring over eight meters is believed to be the stone where she either tethered her boat, or was the actual stone boat in which she sailed. This large stone called the *barca* is the center of the *Romería de la Virgen de la Barca* celebrated from the 13th to the 16th of September. Locals believe that dancers who perform on the stone, and are able to make it move during their performance, will be granted their secret wishes by the natural spirits of the area.

Notker - This Swiss abbot who lived the monastery of St. Gall in Switzerland referred to James's presence in Hispania. Citing the works of Florus de Lyon, 806 - 838, a history of martyrs mention the relics enshrined in Iria Flavia, Notker attested to saint's presence in the Peninsula.

Padrón - A small town located in the Ulla River valley. Padrón's medieval name was Iria Flavia. The village's name may be derived from *Pedrón*, meaning large stone. The lapidary is reportedly kept in the church dedicated to the memory of St. James. Various interpretations exist concerning the origin of the incised stone. Some maintain that the stone formed part of the original crypt of St. James who was buried in Padrón, not Compostela. Others believe that it is the remnant of a Roman temple dedicated to Neptune. During the Roman epoch Padrón was the terminus point of a highway that originated on the shores of the Ebro River in contemporary Zaragoza. Teodomiro, the bishop of this settlement in the 9th century, announced the discovery of the apostle's tomb in 813.

Papal Bull *Omnipotens Deus* - In 1884 Pope Leon XIII proclaimed the authenticity of the remains unearthed in the Cathedral, identifying them to be those of the apostle and his two disciples. The Bull maintained that the burial site contained the remains of a decapitated individual who was flanked by separate tombs that contained the bones of two males.

Pelagio - Different versions of the legendary history named the hermit / shepherd as Pelagio, Pelagius, Pelayo or Paio. He lived in the woods of Libredón and reportedly discovered the tomb of St. James among a grove of oak trees. He witnessed strange lights and heard celestial music in a thicket that contained the ruins of a Roman mausoleum. In some versions he is described as an esthetic, not unlike John, the Baptist.

Petos de ánimas - Located along country roads and crossroads, these stones structures house offerings and written prayers for the dead who wander the byways late at night. Prayers are deposited in these stone boxes for the *almiñas*, lost souls, who are suffering in Purgatory.

Pico Sacro - The site Pico Sacro was where the disciples of James found animals to transport the cart that carried the apostle's sarcophagus. Queen Lupa, the Celtic regent who was suspicious of the disciples, sent them to find draft animals at this site. Instead, they found wild bulls that could only be tamed by the presence of St. James' remains. Local lore maintains that this magical site cured toothaches and other ailments, witches cabals gathered here, and an ancient Roman temple dedicated to Jupiter once stood on this site.

Pórtico de la Gloria - The original medieval facade of the cathedral which contains a pantheon of saints, apostles and figures from the Old and New Testaments stands inside the cathedral's current, outer doors. A British team of art historians severely damaged the polychromed surface of the Pórtico after applying plaster to make castings for the London Museum of Natural History.

Primitus Hispanias convertit dogmate gentes - The first British work, written by an English abbot of the 8th century from Mamesbury, identified James, the Greater, as a participant in the evangelistic effort in the Iberian Peninsula.

Priscillian - This heretical bishop of Avila was decapitated in 385 by the Emperor Maximo. Reportedly born in Iria Flavia in the 4th century, Priscillian was reputed to have practiced a heretical form of Christianity, astrology, and magic once characteristic of the Celts of this region. Regional legend claims that his disciples transported his body from the south of France to Galicia along the route known as the French Way, centuries before the development of the Santiago cult. Some believe that he, not St. James, is buried in the cathedral's crypt of Compostela.

Quintana de Mortos - An ancient cemetery located on the north side of the cathedral, Quintana de Mortos is currently a monumental plaza. The Puerta Santa, the Holy Door to the cathedral, located off of this plaza, is opened for the Jubilee Year. This door was once bricked closed without mortar and opened with a hammer. Recently renovated, the solid door has a cooper interior facade that depicts scenes from the life of St. James.

Qumran - A major theological schism developed between the House of Maccabaeus and a small ultra-religious sect known as the *Hasidim*, the Pious Ones. They established their community in the Wilderness of Qumran and split from mainstream Judaism around 130 BC. This Nazorean or Nazarene sect of the Essenes which had bifurcated from the ancient Hasidim followed an ascetic form of Judaism. The Qumran community began building in the Qumran settlement during the reign of John Hyrcanus in 135 BC.

Régulo - The nemesis of Atanasio and Theodore, Régulo resided in Duyo. Several traditions call him a powerful Christian-hating magician who imprisoned St. James' disciples. Some accounts claim that Régulo was a Roman garrison commander. Others indicate that he was an Austre king or noble. Still other accounts identify the disciples' persecutor as the Roman Legate Filotro who lived in Dugium near Finisterra.

Rías - These coastal inlets were formed by the partial submergence of an unglaciated river valley. These drowned river valleys remained open to the sea forming inlets that line the coast of Galicia, known as the Coast of the Dead.

Rodrigo I - The Visigoth King Rodrigo I failed to prevent the Muslim invasion of the Peninsula at the turn of the 8th century. During an expedition to quell a rebellion in Pamplona, he was apprised of the presence of Muslim forces and hurried south to engage the invaders. The regional disputes and popular dissatisfaction with his rule undermined his military strength and his efforts to turn back the Muslim invaders. Abandoned by the regional Christian commanders, his serfs, and slaves on the eve of battle, King Rodrigo's armies faltered and retreated leaving his kingdom defenseless. Rodrigo's fate is unclear. He either drowned in the Barbate River, site of the battle, or fled this military disaster, leaving only his cape, slippers, and sword.

His abduction and deflowering of Florinda, the daughter of Julian/Yulyan, the Governor of Ceuta proved infortuitous for all of Christian Spain. Yulyan, a Christian Berber who governed Ceuta, sought to avenge the dishonoring of his daughter. Julian's request for revenge coupled with his descriptions of a land rich in natural resources, gold and silver intrigued Musa ibn Nusair. Divided by intrigue and religious disaffection among the oppressed Jewish and Hispano Romano populations, the Christian realm fell quickly to the invaders from the south.

Rodrigo I and Hercules' treasure – Rodrigo I, dissimilar to other Visigoth kings, decided to remove the chains and locks which secured the doors to Hercules' subterranean treasure room. He entered the chamber, only to discover a solitary chest which he ordered to be unlocked. It contained only painted fabric. As the canvas was unfolded a scene began to appear. The city of Toledo was clearly depicted, surrounded by armies whose knights clashed in battle. Torn Christian symbols and banners of Rodrigo's kingdom, broken armaments, and dead warriors appeared in the foreground. Rodrigo ordered the canvass folded and left in the chest and the room sealed for all eternity.

Roman provinces - The five provinces of Tarraconesis, Lusitania, Carthaginensis, Baetica, and Gallaecia comprised the provinces of the Roman Empire in Hispania.

Romería - In the Medieval Latin *romagium* denoted a pilgrimage made to Rome for the purpose of visiting the relics of St. Peter and St. Paul. The common usage of the Spanish *romería* describes a day trip that ends at a sanctuary or hermitage dedicated to the Virgin Mother or a local patron saint. The *romería* may initiate or conclude local or regional celebrations that ultimately have a decidedly secular character. La Romería de la Virgen de la Cabeza in Andújar, Jaén is recognized as the oldest romería pilgrimage of Spain. The romería to Nuestra Señora del Rocío in the village of the Rocío in Almonte, Huelva and the romería of Saint John of the Mountain, celebrated in Miranda de Ebro, are the two most widely attended romerías in Spain.

Romeros - Pilgrims or celebrants who travel to a shrine or sanctuary, a mountain or natural spring during a romería are *romeros*.

The term *rominus, roumius,* or *romeus* was frequently used during the Middle Ages to describe a wanderer or a roamer who traveled from one holy site to another. These pilgrims' continuous ramblings reportedly lacked an apparent, final destination.

Saint Isidoro - San Isidoro, the archbishop of Seville, continued to question the saint's presence and participation in the evangelization of the Peninsula. Only one work attributed to this archbishop located James in Hispania. Finally, Pope Clement VIII of the 16th century expunged all previous references to James's evangelizing in Hispania from the *Brevarium.*

Saint Julian - Saint Julian of Toledo's work of 636 AD, *The Sixth Age,* indicates that the burial site of the martyred James was located in Judea at *Cesarea* of Palestine, an arid region that extends between the delta of the River Nile and the Cirenaica.

Santiago Cult - The cult of Santiago de Compostela began with the discovery of the burial site. Pilgrimage to the church housing his remains began in the 10th century, although local history maintains that local pilgrimage occurred after the discovery of the tomb in the mid to late 800's. St. James' legendary military intervention during the Reconquest added a new dimension to the Santiago cult. Compostela quickly began to challenge Toledo's ecclesiastic role as the religious epicenter of the Christian Spain. The presence of a religious shrine of this magnitude in the northwest corner of Spain forged closer ties with Charlemagne's empire and provided a dynamic religious base of operations for the Christian military campaign during the Reconquest.

Salomé, Maria Helena (Herena) - Salomé was seen as a strong advocate for her sons when she requested that Jesus allow them to sit at his side when he ascended his throne. Mary Helena Salomé occupied a position of importance in the Essene community and possibly bore several names and titles. Identified in some circles as the consort of Zebedee, she held the rank of High Priestess of the Order of Asher and was recognized as a possessor of sacred knowledge. Mary Helena Salomé, a member of the Essene community and follower of its teachings, is believed to have been the first cousin of Mary. Salomé reportedly traveled through the south of France with Mary Magdalen and reached the ancient port of Masillia (Marseilles, France).

Santo dos Croques - The architect Maestro Mateo's kneeling statue is at the base of the Jesse Tree at the entrance of the cathedral. He is forever condemned to do penance facing the main altar for having dared to portray himself alongside the saints and apostles of the *Pórtico de la Gloria*. He is the focus of attention today as tourists and students alike touch their heads to his for wisdom, knowledge, and humility.

The Sar and Sarela Rivers - These two rivers demarcate the location of the city of Santiago de Compostela. *"Entre los ríos Sar y Sarela está Compostela"* is a popular refrain.

Scallop Shell - The symbol of St. James and his *Way*, the scallop shell has been worn by pilgrims down through the ages as a sign of their having completed the pilgrimage route. The symbolism of the scallop may have prehistoric origins, given that it was found in many burial sites of early man in the region. Scallop shells may have symbolized rebirth or a life after death. The shell was seen as a Roman fertility symbol and the birthplace of Venus as she emerged from the sea. Known in Spanish as the *venera* and in Galician *vieira*, the legendary history of St. James mentions the scallop shell in two main episodes of St. James' posthumous return to Spain. The apostle saved the drowning bridegroom and his horse when they inadvertently fell into the sea, their garments encrusted by scallop shells. The ship that returned the martyred James to Spain was described as being covered by scallop shells and barnacles. In medieval paintings, John the Baptist is pictured using this shell to baptize Jesus.

The Silver Route - The *Vía de la Plata*, a contemporary pilgrimage route runs from Andalucía to Galicia and dates back to 3,000 BC when it was a route along which tin, bronze, copper, and other valuable metals flowed. Merchants transported the raw materials to the foundries of ancient Tartessos, located on the Baetis River. This commercial route was a religious-commercial viaduct that spread common cultural and religious components such as the worship of Geryon and, later, Hercules. Clear connections exist between the megalithic Bronze Age Atlantic cultural ark whose commercial network ran along the coast of Portugal into Galicia and the lower river basin of the Guadalquivir.

A substantial tin trade existed between Phoenicia and Carthage and the British Isles during the Bronze and Iron Age. The origin of the word 'Britain' may have been *Baratanak*, a Phoenician denomination for "land of tin." Although the main Phoenician commercial port was Cadiz, it is clear that traders made use of existing maritime and land trade routes between Britain, Tartessos, and Carthage. The northwest corner of the Iberian Peninsula, contemporary Galicia, was central to this commercial intercourse providing a port of entry and a route for the transport of valuable metals. Since silver was not one of the valuable metals transported along this route it may have been known originally as *via lapidata* or route of the stones or a stone lined causeway.

Simancas - Christian forces routed the armies of Abd-er Rahman led by his Slav general, Najda, at the battle of Simancas in 939 AD. St James appeared among the struggling Christian army and reportedly aided their forces in this first victory over the Moors of Al-Andaluz.

Sisnando I - Bishop of Iria Flavia, Sisnando I, with the backing of Alfonso III, built the cathedral that replaced the original church of Alfonso II. Founder of the Monastery of San Fiz, he supported the establishment of the first facility in Santiago that housed and cared for the needs of weary pilgrims.

The Stone of Destiny - The ancient legend of the Stone of Destiny crossed the northwest corner of the Iberian Peninsula millennium ago. The legend recounts that Jacob used the stone as a pillow when he had visions of a ladder that connected the earth with heaven. The stone traveled through Israel, Egypt and, finally, the Iberian Peninsula. The stone passed through Brigantium, ancient city founded by Brath and his son, Breogan. Legend states that this Celtic dynasty crowned its kings on this stone. A prince, Simon Brec from Galicia, was sent with the stone to the isle of Eire, Ireland where it stayed in Tara. In the 5th century, Fergus took the stone to Scotland, enshrining it in the Monastery of Scone, where it became the greatest symbol of Scottish nationhood. King Edward I of England took possession of this artifact and it remained in Westminster abbey until 1996 when the Stone of Destiny was installed in Edinburgh Castle.

Tarik ibn Ziyad - This governor of Tangier crossed the straights of Gibraltar with an invasion force of seven thousand men. Setting his encampment on a site known as Jubal -Tarik (Gibraltar), Tarik attacked the Christian settlements along the coast and fortified his position in this newly acquired territory. On the 19th of July in the year 711, Tarik's Berbers defeated Rodrigo's forces, signaling the beginning of the conquest of Christian Iberia.

Tarraconesis - These northwestern provinces of the Roman Empire included the contemporary cities of Zaragoza, Barcelona and Tarragona.

Tartessos - The Tartessian culture flourished thousands of years before the arrival of the first Phoenician expeditionary force to the Iberian Peninsula. The Tartessians traded with the merchants of King David of Israel and those of the Pharos of Egypt. Tartessos was considered a myth until recent archaeological excavations and biblical scholars placed this famed city firmly in the historical continuum of the Iberian Peninsula. Interestingly enough, contemporary scholars of classic mythology locate the historic battle between Geryon and Hercules (Melqart) not in Galicia, but in the outskirts of Tartessos in the south of Spain. The invading armies led by Melqart disembarked on the Levante coast near Nova Cartago (Cartagena) and met the Tartessian forces of Geryon and the armies of his three sons north of contemporary Sevilla.

The war ended in the destruction of Tartessos, signaling the decline of Tartessian hegemony in the Iberian Peninsula. Melqart's victory assured the ascendancy of Phoenician commercial control, the flourishing of Gades around 9th century BC. These historical conquests found expression in the epic struggle of the Phoenician cultural hero, Melqart with the Tartessian giant, Geryon. With the defeat of Geryon's armies and the fall of Tartessos, Phoenician mercantile interests controlled Tartessian commercial routes and the Peninsula's cultural nexus. Melqart, known by the Romans as Hercules, became the founder of the new political and commercial center, Italica-Hispalis, the twin cities, contemporary Sevilla. Due to the cultural and ethnic cultural flow from Tartessos to the northwestern corner of Spain along the tin trade routes, the mythic battle between the giant Geryon and Hercules was widely disseminated. The legendary accounts took root and became know as an event indigenous to Galicia. The Silver Route further expanded Phoenician cultural and economic hegemony.

Tau - This ancient Hebrew symbol can be seen on the vestments of the statue of St. James in the *Pórtico de la Gloria*. It is traditionally interpreted as signifying acceptance and fulfillment of the word of God. The tau symbol has been related to alchemy and esoteric and metaphysical practices. It is identified as the lower component of the *Cruz de Caravaca* which is associated with the Knights Templars. The tau is considered an example of the syncretism of Eastern and Western religious beliefs.

Templar Knights - The Knights of the Order of the Temple of Jerusalem, a military religious order founded in 1119 in France, contributed to the protection and development of St. James pilgrimage route. The Order's distinct, architectural style is apparent in many of the route's hospitals, public structures, and churches. The Templar presence in Spain was notable during the Reconquest. Ponferrada Castle is an excellent example of Templar architecture.

Teodomiro - His announcement of the discovery of St. James' burial site to King Alfonso II in 813 signaled the official recognition of the existence of the apostle's relics in Galicia. Bishop of Iria Flavia, he established Compostela as the primary religious center for his Episcopal seat. Upon hearing of the sighting, Theodomiro, decided to fast for three days before beginning the investigation. His Episcopal seat was located 17 kilometers from the discovery site in Iria Flavia. Accompanied by local priests, he visited and ordered the excavation of the site. The bishop traveled to Oviedo, the capital of the Asturian kingdom, and reported the discovery to the king, Alfonso II, the Chaste.

Tiraboleiros - These eight men are assigned the task of swinging the *botafumeiro* during the feast days and special religious days of the Compostelano liturgical calendar. To date, there have been only four reported accidents with the *botafumeiro*. Once, the incense burner flew out the Platerías Door, landed on the Rúa do Vilar, and reportedly killed a chestnut seller.

Torte of Santiago - Compostela's signature torte made with lemon rinds and crushed almonds. The Cross of Santiago is etched in red food coloring, frosted with confectionary sugar, and is served with sweet wine. Known as the *tarta de Santiago,* free samples are given out along the streets of Santiago de Compostela.

Toulouse, France - Toulouse claimed to have the remains of St. James before King Alfonso II announced to Pope Leo III and Charlemagne that the saint's remains had been found in Galicia.

Traslatio - The transfer of St. James' remains to a more suitable and secure location was denoted by the term traslatio.

Ultreya/Ultreia - Meaning *Onward,* medieval pilgrims shouted this exclamation when they saw the bell towers of the Cathedral visible from behind the walls of the city. The pilgrims voiced this sigh of relief as they headed down Monte del Gozo towards the outskirts of Compostela.

Via Caesar Augusta - This ancient Roman highway system crossed the Peninsula, running from Zaragoza to the southwestern city of Mérida.

Virgen del Pilar - Mary, the mother of Jesus, reportedly appeared to the crestfallen James as she approached the western shore of Galicia in a small boat. After this Marian vision, the craft miraculously transformed into stone. Mary revitalized and encouraged the apostle to continue his work among the pagans. She appeared once again to the apostle on the banks of the Ebro River in the year 40 AD. The Virgin encouraged him not to lose faith and instructed him to build a chapel in her honor at the sight where angels would descend among flashes of light. The Virgin appeared and either alighted upon a column of stone, or placed a wooden or stone statuette of her likeness on a column of jasper. She requested that James build a chapel to house this *Virgen del Pilar,* the Virgin of the Pillar.

Way of St. James - A series of pilgrimage routes traverse the Iberian Peninsula and culminate in the northwestern corner of Spain. Pilgrimage to St. James' tomb has been a Christian tradition since the 10th century and shares equal importance with the pilgrimage sites of Rome and Jerusalem. The Augustinian and Cluny religious orders fomented travel to the shrine, financed, and oversaw the construction of inns, hospitals, and monasteries along the route.

Zebedee - A fisherman by trade who lived with his two sons and wife on the shores of Genesareth, Zebedee was a prominent figure in the Essene community. St. Jerome indicates that James' family was from Joppa and "of noble origin." This may have referred to his family ties with Jesus, heir to King David's throne. In *Butler's Lives of the Saints,* Zebedee is identified as a fisherman by trade who lived with his two sons and wife on the shores of Genesareth. Recognized as a minister of the sanctuary, he would have participated in ceremonies that symbolized the struggle between the cosmic forces of Light and Darkness. The term *boanerges,* frequently associated with his sons, James and John, may have been a reference to the prestige and power that Zebedee held in the Essene community, and thus the term, *sons of thunder.* Affiliated with the Zealots, he reportedly participated in an unsuccessful revolt during the rule of Pontius Pilate. Zebedee's political activism led to his excommunication by Herod Agrippa I. Sources mention his membership in the Sicarii, a group of Jewish assassins who attacked prominent Hellenized and Romanized Jews during the time of the Second Temple. Other accounts credit Zebedee with the demise of Herod Agrippa; a painful death by poisoning. However, it is worth noting that the Sicarii were most active around 48 AD and were most likely not the authors of Agrippa's death in 44 AD.

BIBLIOGRAPHY

Aguilera, Francisco Enrique. *Santa Eulaia's People: Ritual structure and progress in an Andalucian community.* Illinois: Waveland Press, 1978.

Alarcón, Rafael H. *A la sombra de los templarios.* Barcelona: Ediciones Martínez Roca, S.A., 1986.

Allardyce, Isabel. *Historic Shrines of Spain.* New York: Franciscan Missionary Press, 1912.

Allegro, J.M. *The Dead Sea Scrolls.* Baltimore: Penguin Books Inc., 1957.

Aracil, Miguel. *Guía mágica del camino de Santiago.* Barcelona: Ediciones Indio, 1991.

Atienza, Juan. *Los enclaves templarios.* Barcelona: Martínez Roca, 1995.

Aveni, Anthony. *Empires of Time.* New York. Basic Books, Inc., 1989.

Baigent, Michael, Leigh, Richard & Henry Lincoln. *Holy Blood, Holy Grail.* New York: Dell Publishing, 1983. *The Messianic Legacy.* New York: Dell Publishing, 1986.

Begg, Ean. *The Cult of the Black Virgin.* Arkana: Penguin Books, 1996.

Bendiner, Elmer. *The Rise and Fall of Paradise: When Arabs and Jews built a Kingdom in Spain.* New York: Dorset Press, 1983.

Bravo Lozano, Millán. *Guía práctica del peregrino: El Camino de Santiago.* Madrid: Editorial Everest, S.A., 1995.

Brownrigg, Ronald. *The Twelve Apostles.* New York: MacMillan Co., 1974.

Campbell, Joseph. *Occidental Mythology: The Masks of God.* New York: Penguin Books, 1964.

Carr, Raymond and Fusi, Juan Pablo. *Spain: Dictatorship to Democracy.* London: George Allen & Unwin, 1979.

Crow, John. *The Root and the Flower.* Berkeley: University of California Press, 1985.

Castro, Americo. *Realidad Histórica de España.* México: Editorial Porrua, S.A., 1962.

España en su Historia: Cristianos, Moros y Judios. Buenos Aires: Editorial Losada, S.A. 1948.

Davies, Horton and Marie-Helene, Lewisburg. *Holy Days and Holidays: The Medieval Pilgrimage to Compostela.* New York: Bucknell University Presses, 1982.

Díaz- Andreu, Margarita and Keay, Simon. *The Archaeology of Iberia: Dynamics of Change.* London: Routledge Press, 1977.

Dunn, Maryjane and Davidson, Linda Kay. *The Pilgrimage to Compostela in the Middle Ages: A Book of Essays.* London: Garland Publishing, Inc. 1996.

Eliade, Mircea. *The Sacred and the Profane: The Nature of Religion.* New York: Harcourt Brace Jovanovich, 1959.

Eisenman, Robert. *James the Brother of Jesus.* New York: Penguin Books, 1997.

Feinber, Ellen. *Following the Milky Way.* Iowa: Iowa State University Press, 1989.

Ferreiro, Alberto. *The Cult of Saints and Divine Patronage in Gallaecia before Santiago. The Pilgrimage to Santiago in the Middle Ages; A Book of Essays.* Dunn and Davidson.

Fraguas, Antonio. *Santiago de Compostela.* Madrid: Publicaciones Españolas, 1976.

Franco Taboada, Arturo. *Los orígenes de Compostela: Una historia dibujada.* La Coruña: Excma. Diputación Provincial de la Coruña, 1987.

Gardner, Laurence. *Bloodline of the Holy Grail.* New York: Barnes & Noble Books, 1996.

Giner de los Ríos, Gloria & R. de García Lorca, Laura. *Cumbres de la civilización española.* New York: Holt, Rinehart and Winston, 1966.

Gitlitz, David & Davidson, Linda Kay. *The Pilgrimage Road to Santiago.* New York: St. Martin's Griffin, 2000.

Grant, Michael. Jesus: *An Historian's Review of the Gospels.* New York: Charles Scribner, 1977. *The History of Ancient Israel.* New York: Charles Scribner, 1984.

Hadingham, Evan. *Early Man and the Cosmos.* Walker Co., 1984. *Lines to the Mountain Gods.* New York: Random House, 1987.

Hartman, Louis. *Lives of the Saints 2nd Volume.* New York: John Crowley & Co., 1963.

Haskins, Susan. *Mary Magdalen: Myth and Metaphor.* New York: The Berkley Publishing Co., 1993.

Herm, Gerhard. *The Celts.* New York: St. Martin's Press, 1975.

Kamen, Henry. *A Concise History of Spain.* New York: Charles Scribner's Sons, 1973.

Kendall, Alan. *Medieval Pilgrims: The Wayland Documentary History Series.* New York: Wayland Publishers, 1970.

Knight, Christopher & Lomas, Robert. *The Second Messiah.* Boston: Element Books, Inc., 1997.

Korb, Scott. *Life in Year One.* New York. Riverhead Books, 2010.

Lozan, Millán Bravo. *Guía práctica del peregrino: El camino de Santiago.* Barcelona: Editorial Everest, S.A., 1995.

Maalouf, Amin. *Las cruzadas vistas por los árabes.* Madrid: Alianza Editorial, 1989.

Mackay, Angus. *Atlas of Medieval Europe.* London: Routledge, 1997.

MacMullen, Ramsay. *Christianity and Paganism in the Fourth to Eighth Centuries.* New Haven: Yale University Press, 1997.

McCauley, Lucy. *Spain: The Stories of Life on the Road*. New York: Traveler's Tales, Inc., 1998.

Mohen, Jean-Pierre. *Megaliths: Stones of Memory*. New York: Harry N. Abrams, Inc. 1999.

Montenegro, Angel. *Historia de España: Colonizaciones y Formación de los Pueblos Preromanos*. Madrid: Editorial Gredos, 1989.

Munro, Eleanor. *On Glory Roads: A Pilgrim's Book about Pilgrimage*. New York: Thames & Hudson, 1987.

O'Grady, Joan. *Early Christian Heresies*. New York: Barnes and Noble Books, 1985.

Patai, Raphael. *The Jewish Alchemists: A History and Source Book*. Princeton: Princeton University Press, 1994.

Reames, Sheryl L. *The Legenda Aurea: A Reexamination of Its Paradoxical History*. Madison: The University of Wisconsin Press, 1985.

Ricci, Carla. Mary *Magdalene and Many Others: Women who Followed Jesus*. Minneapolis: First Fortress Press, 1994.

Robinson, Martin. *Sacred Places, Pilgrim Paths: An Anthology of Pilgrimage*. London: Harper Collins Publishers, 1997.

Roob, Alexander. *Alchemy and Mysticism*. London: Taschen, 1997.

Rudgley, Ricahrd. *The Lost Civilizations of the Stone Age*. New York: Simon and Schuster, 1999.

Ryan, Granger and Ripperger, Helmut. *The Golden Legend of Jacobus de Voragine*. New York: Arno Press, 1969.

Shreeve, James. *The Neandertal Enigma: Solving the Mystery of Modern Human Origins*. New York: William Morrow & Co., Inc., 1995.

Silver, Daniel Jeremy. *A History of Judaism*. Basic Books, Inc., 1974.

Stanton, Edward. *Road of Stars to Santiago*. Kentucky: University Press of Kentucky, 1994.

Stark, Rodney. *The Rise of Christianity: A Sociologist Reconsiders History*. Princeton: Princeton University Press, 1996.

Starkie, Walter. *The Road to Santiago*. Berkeley: University of California Press, 1965.

Stokstad, Marilyn. *Santiago de Compostela: In the Age of the Great Pilgrimages*. Oklahoma City: University of Oklahoma Press, 1978.

The Jerome Bible Commentary. New York: Prentice Hall, 1968.

The Jerusalem Bible. New York: Doubleday, 1966.

Thurston, Herbert and Attwater, Donald. *Butler's Lives of the Saints*. London: University Press, 1956.

Tuñón de Lara, Manuel. *Historia de España: Introducción, Primeras Culturas e Hispania Romana*. Barcelona: Editorial Labor, S.A., 1982.

Ugarte, Francisco. *España y su civilización*. New York: Odyssey Press, 1965.

Valdeavellano, G.de, Luis. *Historia de España*. Madrid: Revista de Occidente, S.A., 1952.

Wilson, Colin. *Starseekers*. New York: Doubleday & Co., 1980.

Young, Dudley. *Origins of the Sacred: The Ecstasies of Love and War*. New York: St. Martin's Press, 1991.